Hope Transformed

A Battle Strategy for Surviving Life's Greatest Trials

JOY CRUSE

Contributed by Tait Cruse and edited by Marya Lewis

WESTBOW
PRESS
A DIVISION OF THOMAS NELSON

All Scripture quotations, unless otherwise noted, are taken from the New International Version, copyright 1973, 1978, 1984 by the International Bible Society.

WestBow Press books may be ordered through booksellers or by contacting:

WestBow Press
A Division of Thomas Nelson
1663 Liberty Drive
Bloomington, IN 47403
www.westbowpress.com
1-(866) 928-1240

Library of Congress Control Number: 2011961084

ISBN: 978-1-4497-3245-5 (hc)
ISBN: 978-1-4497-3244-8 (sc)
ISBN: 978-1-4497-3243-1 (e)

Printed in the United States of America

WestBow Press rev. date: 12/20/2011

This book is dedicated to Connor Cruse. He is truly my hero! As our friend Matt Goodwin said about Connor....

The strength of a boy staring fear in the eye;
Courage that few will ever know;
Never backing down, never giving in;
A flame that burned brightly, but for a moment;
A true champion for Christ.

"Well done good and faithful servant."
Matthew 25:23

Contents

Foreword

Praise be to the God and Father of our Lord Jesus Christ! In his great mercy he has given us new birth into a living hope through the resurrection of Jesus Christ from the dead—
1 Peter 1:3

Hope is the living reality of life in Christ. So much more than wishful thinking, hope is the confident assurance that our lives are in God's hands. Hope is the ultimate security. We discover this sure expectation in our relationship with Jesus Christ.

It is impossible to survive life's greatest challenges without this eternal hope. Joy and Tait Cruse were faced with the unthinkable—their precious four-year-old son, Connor, was diagnosed with an aggressive pediatric cancer, and suddenly, the Cruse family was in a no-holds-barred fight for Connor's life. This incredible family would never be the same.

As their pastor, neighbor, and friend, I watched Joy and Tait relentlessly pursue every possibility to save Connor's life for four years. The finest medical knowledge and treatment was applied. Yet, in the midst of this tragedy, I saw a couple, united in Christ, holding strong together and never, ever giving up. Joy and Tait especially never gave up on their hope in Christ. In spite of devastating events, disappointments, and setbacks, they kept their focus on God. They walked in the Spirit. They filled their minds with God's Word. *They turned to faith for friends in their church.* They sheltered themselves in Jesus' loving care.

I am so glad Joy and Tait preserved their journey of pain, suffering, and faith in *Hope Transformed*. The comfort this godly couple received, they now share with us. This account is soaked with tears, but it is not without hope.

You need this book. If not now, you will, because all of us will face seasons of suffering in life. That's when we need more than optimism. What we need is hope. This book will lift your soul into the presence of God. You will discover in these pages the strength to hold on to hope and never quit. You will find a faith that lives and refuses to give up what we know for what we don't know. And what we know is that Jesus is Lord, and there is always hope in Him.

The Rev. Jack Graham
Lead Pastor, Prestonwood Baptist Church, Plano, Texas

Endorsements
for *Hope Transformed*

"This book describes the journey of loving hearts through the valley of the shadow of death and how they find joy, share love, and emerge with hope. I've rarely observed a more honest portrayal of raw human emotion met by God's grace expressed in ways that offer such comfort and strength. *Hope Transformed* provides expression for anguished souls, perspective for life's unanswered mysteries, and substance for faith. It sheds the tears of the brokenhearted and declares the faithfulness of God."

—Dr. David McKinley, Senior Pastor, Warren Baptist Church, Augusta, GA, and author of *The Life You Were Born to Give*

"*Hope Transformed* is more than a compelling true story of the Cruse family. It is a map for the rest of us to use when facing the toughest challenges of life. It is full of wisdom and insights, and it presents a unique paradigm for redefining hope."

—Steve Stroope, Lead Pastor, Lake Pointe Church, Rockwall, TX

"Both Kim (my wife) and I were very moved by the Cruses' story. The strength of their faith, especially in light of everything they went through, is an inspiration to both of us. More than once, we have said that whenever we need some hope or some sign from God, we will turn back to this book. It meant that much to us. This book is a great reminder that our hope doesn't come from what we do, but from Jesus Christ. It's so easy for us in this new corporate role to forget that—with this book I'm sure we never will."

—John Schlifske, CEO and Chairman
of Northwestern Mutual Financial Network

"*Hope Transformed* is not just about two parents and their greatest fear. It is a story of real, raw, authentic faith and the Cruses' walk with God through the valley of death. Tait and Joy Cruse inspire me—not because of what they say but by the way they live and the faith they have. I encourage you to read this book and let their lives, their faith, and their son Connor touch your heart and soul."

—Jon Gordon, best-selling author of *The Energy Bus* and *Soup*

"'What gives you hope?' It's the question that Karen and I sought the answer to after we lost our son. *Hope Transformed* is a compelling account of the greatest challenge a parent can face, but its pages are filled with wisdom and encouragement for anyone searching for hope. You will be forever changed by the story of Connor Cruse, whose life was truly a portrait of God's transforming love."

—Rick Santorum, 2012 US presidential candidate and former
US senator from Pennsylvania

Acknowledgements...

MacKenzie, Carson and Mason
I'm thankful for the sweet gift of you. You all have dealt with so much at such a young age. I watched you bravely handle all the chaos and fear that came with Connor's cancer. Many times, Mom and Dad were at the hospital when you needed us and we watched you grow up from afar. The loss of Connor has also been life changing, and now you are dealing with this grief. My prayer for you is that God would use this journey with Connor to grow and mature you into something beautiful. Thank you for adding fun, laughter, frustration, depth, joy and love into my life.

Mom and Lexie
You both loved Connor so well! You always held his hand when he needed comfort or strength. You prayed with him when he was scared. You made him laugh when he was sad. You laughed when he was his crazy, silly self. You loved him when he needed love and you cried with us when he went to be with his Heavenly Father.

Marya Lewis
Thank you for putting all these journal entries into the format of a book. Without your direction and your help, I know this book would never have come to fruition. Thank you for your help, love, encouragement and friendship!

Tait

We have traveled together through this dark journey of childhood cancer and losing our son. I want to thank you for your support of me, Connor and our family. We needed a spiritual leader and a warrior to fight for Connor and to hold us together as a family. God chose the right person to be my husband and to be Connor's dad. Navigating through all this is not for the faint of heart, and you have truly become the strong tower that our family needed. I know that we will always miss our sweet ConCon, but together we can love each other, cling to God and watch as God brings beauty from these ashes. I love you.

Much love, support and prayers came from our extended family, Prestonwood Baptist Church, Prestonwood Christian Academy and Northwestern Mutual Financial Network. Thank you and thanks to all of you who prayed faithfully for Connor and our family over the last six years.

Introduction

Hope—it is a word I rarely used in the first half of my life. I suppose I had it filed away in my vocabulary alongside words like *wish* and *dream*. But on a spring afternoon in 2005, I found myself scrambling to understand the word that would define the next four years of my life. On Sunday, May 15, at 4:00 p.m., my husband and I learned that our four-year-old son, Connor, had cancer. The news hit my heart like an earthquake. But the shockwaves continued: Connor had neuroblastoma, a form of pediatric cancer that begins with an initial tumor but multiplies quickly as it travels through the sympathetic nervous system.

I remember scanning the faces of the doctors surrounding us, searching for a hint of positivity, a sign of optimism, a glimmer of *hope*, but there was none. The doctors sentenced our son to three agony-filled months to live. My head was spinning, and yet, in that moment, a small part of my brain was disconnecting from this grim diagnosis. I stopped listening to the doctors and began devising my own plan of hope—a plan to keep my son alive.

Hope Transformed is the story of how this plan began and ended. It is a record of our journey from fragile hope in our son's healing to complete hope and total trust in the only One who can truly meet all our needs, Jesus Christ. We want you to know that this is not just a book about battling cancer—it is a book about the battles we all face as a result of living in a fallen world. Divorce, illness, bankruptcy, the loss of a loved one, the end of a relationship: each of these trials can leave us battered and stripped of courage and hope. Yet here we stand, on the other side of tragedy, and we can tell you that we have not lost hope. Our hope has just been readjusted, *transformed*.

It is from our position post-tragedy that we can offer you these words of encouragement: no matter what type of devastation you have faced, are facing now, or will face in the future, there is wisdom to be gained and joy to be discovered in the deepest valleys of life. Extracting these gifts from hardship, however, requires willingness to surrender our needs and desires to the perfect will of God. It is only after this exchange that we will experience the peace that comes from complete trust in a loving heavenly Father.

So where is your hope today? Have you placed it in your own abilities? In the hands of doctors? In the counsel of friends? If you are unsure, we invite you inside our personal journey, into the raw emotions, the valleys, and the great victories we experienced during our fight for Connor's life. Within each chapter of *Hope Transformed*, you will find anecdotes and reflections that point you to the healing truths of God's Word.

We pray that your trust in God will grow as you read and learn to release your pain, worries, and despair into the competent hands of the Great Comforter.

God bless you,
Joy and Tait Cruse

Chapter 1

D-Day

For several days, Connor complained of a recurring stomachache and ran a slight fever—*nothing a little Tylenol® can't help*, I told myself. When Connor's complaints persisted, we visited our family doctor and left his office with the assurance that Connor probably had some type of stomach flu. My husband, Tait, and I agreed that if Connor wasn't feeling better by the weekend, we would take him to the emergency room. I was convinced he had a problem with his appendix.

When Connor awoke on Sunday morning in tears from his stomach pain, I drove him to Children's Medical Center in Dallas while Tait stayed home with our other two children. The doctors ran several tests, including an X-ray and a CAT scan. By 4:00 that afternoon, I was getting weary (I was five months pregnant with our son Mason at the time), so Tait joined me at the hospital while a friend watched the children. By early evening, a team of doctors approached us in the waiting area with Connor's test results and a diagnosis. They were 99 percent sure that Connor had neuroblastoma. *Neuroblastoma?* Tait and I stared at each other and then at Connor. We were unfamiliar with this ominous-sounding word. One of the doctors explained that it was a type of pediatric cancer. As we began calling family members and friends to ask for prayer, the waiting room soon filled with familiar faces. Deacons and elders from a church we had not yet joined came to sit with us. Neighbors, friends, and our children's teachers surrounded us, offering words of comfort and encouragement. But as more doctors gathered, huddling like football players trying to figure out the next play, my hopes were diminishing.

I did my best to conceal my emotions from Connor as we waited for the oncologist to deliver more information on the severity of his condition. I took Connor into the gift shop to distract him from the chaos around him. When he selected a toy robot, I nodded in approval. His little face lit up with excitement. As I cherished this quiet moment, the oncologist's return cut through our momentary respite like a knife. Nothing could have prepared me for what he would say: Connor had stage four advanced neuroblastoma. The primary tumor consisted of a nine-centimeter mass throughout his stomach, but the cancer had already metastasized to the bones in his legs, his shoulders, his pelvis, and his ribs. There were smaller tumors behind his heart and around his spine. Upon hearing this horrible news, Tait's knees buckled, and a friend caught him before he hit the floor. I couldn't speak or move. I stood motionless, paralyzed with sensory overload.

As we watched this unwanted drama unfold, visions of our son playing high school baseball, going to college, even getting married, were becoming foggy. To make things worse, the doctors' discussions of emergency surgery to remove the primary tumor were halted by the ominous word *inoperable*. With no concrete decisions made, the doctors left for the night, and we were admitted to our first hospital room at Children's Medical Center. At 9:00 p.m., the last group of our friends left, assuring us they would return in the morning. There we were—alone with our thoughts, a beeping machine, and our bewildered four-year-old son. These were our first six hours of living with cancer. This was our "D-day"—diagnosis day.

Perhaps you have had a D-day: a day of unexpected pain or loss, a day that produced a detour sign in the path you had envisioned for your life. When these days occur, we are immediately faced with a critical choice: fade into the shadows of despair or stand up and fight. Perhaps it was the motherly instinct inside me, but from the moment of Connor's diagnosis, I entered battle mode. Anger welled inside me, and I told myself that I would challenge anyone or anything that stood in the way of my son's healing.

Yet in the pre-dawn hours, as I watched my precious boy sleeping, my tears flowed freely. I secretly wondered if I had enough courage and strength to endure this trial. As I thought of my other children, my parents, and my close friends, I wondered what changes this ordeal would bring for them. Most of all I thought of Connor. How would I explain why he had suddenly become so sick when I didn't know the answer myself?

Weary from the events of the day, I bowed my head to pray. I cried out to the God of my childhood—the God I'd learned of in Sunday school, the God who performed miracles in the Bible. I needed that God to hear my prayer. I asked Him to reach down from heaven and heal my son. I truly believed God was capable of performing such a miracle. (I still do!) However, as I drifted in and out of restless sleep, doubts plagued my mind and fear surfaced in my heart.

Faithfulness

> *Yet this I call to mind and therefore I have hope: Because of the Lord's great love we are not consumed, for His compassions never fail. They are new every morning; great is your faithfulness.*
>
> —Lamentations 3:21-23

It is still difficult to look back to that first night of diagnosis in the ER. Actually, Tait and I can't even talk about it. Remembering that night brings the darkest of emotions crashing down on me. I don't think I've ever felt so raw. I kept waking up on a fold-out couch in the hospital to find that my nightmare was indeed real.

But as I stand here today, looking back over the past four years—the scary times, the difficult times, and the heartbreaking times—I realize that one thing remained constant: God never left our side. He carried us through our dark journey. He gave us hope when the doctors offered none. He gave Connor vitality when, according to the medical reports, he should have been fragile, sickly, and tired. God gave us strength when we had nothing left. He gave us answers to our prayers and blessings along the way. He showed us kindness through our friends, family, and strangers. He gave us encouragement through His Word. He gave our son four years of life when all the odds said he should have died within three months.

Trials always test our patience. But when they come (and they will), there is an important issue we must settle in our hearts. We have to learn how to separate God's faithfulness (which never fails or ends) from our desire to receive a specific answer from Him. So many times I was tempted to question God's faithfulness when we received bad test results. And then I discovered this verse:

> Shadrach, Meshach and Abednego replied to the king, "O Nebuchadnezzar, we do not need to defend ourselves before you in this matter. If we are thrown into the blazing furnace, the God we serve is able to save us from it, and he will rescue us from your hand, O king. But

even if he does not, we want you to know, O king, that
we will not serve your gods or worship the image of gold
you have set up" (Daniel 3:16-18).

Having the faith that Shadrach, Meshach, and Abednego displayed
requires absolute trust in God's faithfulness *and* His perfect will for
our lives.

Overwhelmed

> *We were under great pressure, far beyond our ability to endure, so that we despaired even of life. Indeed, in our hearts we felt the sentence of death. But this happened that we might not rely on ourselves but on God, who raises the dead.*
> —2 Corinthians 1:8-10

During the worst trials, it is easy to become overwhelmed. The burden of our pain seems too great, and the potential for disaster looms too close to home. As we struggle to process our devastation, questions flood our minds: *Did God think I could endure this? Did He think my loved one could endure this?*

The truth is that we're not supposed to walk through trials in our own strength. Instead, we are to rely fully on God's strength as the verse above explains. The Bible is filled with profiles of God's people in impossible situations. With two million freed slaves trusting him to find God's Promised Land, Moses faced the Red Sea. Armed with a hammer, nails, and God's message, Noah began the monumental task of constructing the ark. Gripping his faith, Daniel stared into a pit of hungry lions. At the age of one hundred, Abraham struggled to hold back his emotions as he considered holding a newborn son in his hands.

As I faced my own impossible situation, I prayed constantly for sources of comfort and relief. In one of my many overwhelmed moments, I came across these words from the hymn, "Guide Me, O Thou Great Jehovah": "Guide me, O Thou great Jehovah, pilgrim through this barren land; I am weak, but Thou art mighty; hold me with Thy powerful hand . . . Open now the crystal fountain, whence the healing stream doth flow; let the fire and cloudy pillar lead me all my journey through; strong deliverer, be Thou still my strength and shield."[1]Are you allowing God to be your strength and shield? Perhaps you have relinquished part of your current struggle to God, but you are still partially relying on your own strength. What will it take for you to trust Him completely?

It Isn't Fair

I am the Lord your God, who teaches you what is best for you,
who directs you in the way you should go.

—Isaiah 48:17

When our Bible study class studied the book of Job, many of the verses hit home with me—especially the portions where Job seeks to understand why God allowed him to experience such devastation. It is natural to want to understand the purpose of our trials. When Connor was in pain and was not able to participate in simple activities with his friends, I struggled with the unfairness of it all. It seemed too much for a child to bear for half his life—the only part that he really remembered.

Of course there were moments when I became angry and distant. If we were going to walk down this road, I thought I deserved to know why. In one of my periods of searching for answers, I discovered this quote from Alfred Edersheim:

"We cannot understand the meaning of man's trials; God does not explain them. To explain a trial would be to destroy its objective, which is that of calling forth simple faith and implicit obedience. If we knew why the Lord sent us this or that trial, it would thereby cease to be a trial either of faith or patience."[2]

I guess at one time or another, we are all called to share in the suffering of Christ, all the while realizing that our pain cannot compare to what Christ actually suffered.

If you feel trapped in the "why me" stage of your struggle, I encourage you to look past the questions and the feelings of injustice. While you may not understand the purpose of your trial at this point, you can be certain that God will work *all* things—even your current situation—to your good and for His glory (Romans 8:28).

Temporal

> *And call upon me in the day of trouble: I will deliver thee,*
> *and thou shalt glorify me.*
>
> —Psalm 50:15

Following is a journal entry I wrote: late at night in my home office during the first month of Connor's treatment. These journal entries were on our blog and were written to the many people (a few thousand) following Connor's journey. We had family members and friends reading these journal entries. There were also fellow church members, families from school, and people we didn't even know who followed Connor's story.

> Tait is at the hospital spending the night with Connor, so I get a little free time while the kids are asleep. Connor did great today. He actually ate a picnic with his friends from Bible study and then played on the playground for an hour. Later, he played in his hospital room with some friends from our old neighborhood. The reason I tell you this is because we rejoice in every little bit of good news, and it is so good to see him get out of bed and interact with his friends.
>
> I wanted to tell you all how grateful I am for your prayers, support, encouragement, meals, and visits. Connor especially wants to thank you for the toys you've brought him. I'm overwhelmed by your outpouring of love. It's amazing what God's family can do when we pull together like this. I want to leave you with a couple of verses that have helped me over the last few months. When I think about Connor and how his little body is suffering—vomiting, nosebleeds, losing weight, losing his hair, etc., I think of this verse: "Therefore we do not lose heart. Though outwardly we are wasting away, yet inwardly we are being renewed day by day. For our light and momentary troubles are achieving for us an eternal

glory that far outweighs them all. So we fix our eyes not on what is seen, but on what is unseen, since what is seen is temporary, but what is unseen is eternal" (2 Corinthians 4:16-18).

I try to remember that we are here on earth for God's glory, and Connor will be used to bring glory to God. I try to focus on that and remain grateful that God is using Connor in such a mighty way. "My grace is sufficient for you, for my power is made perfect in weakness. Therefore, I will boast all the more gladly about my weaknesses, so that Christ's power may rest on me. That is why, for Christ's sake, I delight in weaknesses, insults, hardships, persecutions, and difficulties. For when I am weak, then I am strong" (2 Corinthians 12:9-10).

The Issue of Uncertainty

> *Dear friends, now we are children of God, and what we will be has not yet been made known. But we know that when Christ appears, we shall be like Him, for we shall see Him as He is.*
>
> —1 John 3:2

Even though we've lived in the same town for five years, I find comfort in having GPS in my car so that I can see what's ahead. There is something unnerving about not knowing what is around the next corner of the road. It is even more stressful to wonder what is ahead on the path of life.

Many times during Connor's illness, uncertainty emerged as the primary source of my anxiety. The countless hours we spent in waiting rooms, labs, and doctors' offices drained my courage and threatened my resolve. In a devotion titled "The Graciousness of Uncertainty," Oswald Chambers captures this emotion.

"Naturally, we are inclined to be so mathematical and calculating that we look upon uncertainty as a bad thing. We imagine that we have to reach some end, but that is not the nature of spiritual life . . . 'Believe also in Me,' said Jesus, not—'Believe certain things about Me.' Leave the whole thing to Him. It is gloriously uncertain how He will come in, but He will come. Remain loyal to Him."[3]

When faced with uncertainty, it is easy to become weary from trying to guess what the future holds. Often, I would formulate a plan in my head on how I would react to different scenarios. Ironically, nothing ever happened the way I imagined or predicted. In the end, I found it much more productive to focus on Christ and His love for me than to focus on my circumstances or uncertainties. Resting in Him was the only way to travel up this steep, rugged path shrouded with uncertainty. I had to Force myself to not look behind or ahead of me. I had to focus on Christ and trust that He would equip me for the journey ahead.

Searching for Answers

23 Let us hold unswervingly to the hope we profess, for He who promised is faithful.—Hebrews 10:23

In the movie *Bruce Almighty*, Jim Carrey is temporarily granted the powers and abilities of God. One of his new responsibilities is answering prayers, which he receives and processes via e-mail. Wow! How great would it be to receive an e-mail from God with the answers to our prayer requests? I have spent many sleepless nights wondering why we were not receiving immediate answers to our countless prayers for Connor.

Author Sarah Young provides an excellent reminder that God is indeed always listening to and working on our requests. In *Jesus Calling*, she states, "When you bring Me prayer requests, lay out your concerns before Me. Speak to Me candidly; pour out your heart. Then thank Me for the answers that I have set into motion long before you can discern results."[4]

Isn't that an incredible thought? The God of the universe wants us to come to Him with our concerns. Not only that, but out of His great love for us, He has already created a perfect set of answers that He will reveal in His perfect timing. But there is one more point we should not miss: we must maintain a spirit of thankfulness toward God while we wait for His answers. Even when we do not know what hardships lie ahead, even when we don't know why God is leading us down a particular path, He wants us to be thankful. Certainly it is tempting to feel insecure when answers don't come according to our timetable. But we must hold fast to the confession of our hope. In uncertain times, it is especially important to hold on to our hope in Christ. How else can we carry on?

Thanksgiving

> *I have come that they may have life, and have it to the full.*
> —John 10:10

My perspective on thanksgiving will forever be changed. In the past, I was always thankful during the good times, when it was easy to be thankful. Now I'm starting to understand how to be thankful during the difficult times. When I look hard enough, I can see that God has placed little blessings along the way to encourage me and bring me closer to Him. I've often said that Tait and I have a front row seat to see what God is going to do through all of this. We will see His glory firsthand if we just keep our eyes open.

That is the one request that Moses asked of God in Exodus 33:13-19 (author's paraphrase). He wanted to see God's Glory. Moses said to Him,

> You can call me by name and tell me I have found favor with You. Please, if this is really so, show me Your intentions so I will understand You more fully and do exactly what You want me to do." And the Lord replied, "I will personally go with you, Moses. I will give you rest—everything will be fine for you."
>
> Then Moses said, "If You don't go with us personally, don't let us move a step from this place." Then Moses had one more request. "Please let me see your glorious presence."
>
> The Lord replied, "I will make all My goodness pass before you. I will call out My name to you. I will show kindness and mercy to you. I will show you My glory."

I want the same thing that Moses did. I want to see God's glory. As Moses said, if God is with me, I can move forward. I will know more fully what I am to do and I will have rest. When I see His glory (blessings) as I travel through this long journey, it will help me carry on.

Tait and I can feel our spiritual lives deepening and growing. My sister-in-law, Christie, told us that we have been given a gift in that we are able to see everything clearer now. We are no longer weighed down by all the frivolous worries in life. Our focus has become singular: seeking God at all times. I hope that we will continue to focus on the important things, to live life the way God intended us to, and to appreciate every moment God has given us.

Chapter 2

Building a War Chest

Perhaps you've heard of Bear Grylls, the star of Discovery Channel's *Man vs. Wild*. The premise of the show is that Bear struggles to survive extreme wilderness situations using only the contents of his pockets and his natural abilities. His efforts are admirable, and by the end of each program, he has battled the elements and emerged victorious.

In the wilderness of our own trials, it is natural to first draw from our own resources to solve our problems. We sit down at our computers, cell phones in hand, and feel that we are invincible—any problem can be solved through an Internet search, right? While there is nothing wrong with a diligent attempt to remove a problem from our lives, we are bound to encounter hardships that just can't be resolved by our own strength. After receiving Connor's diagnosis, we were left with the daunting task of determining the best course of treatment for him. I wasn't sure if God expected us to find the right course of treatment for Connor on our own, but I couldn't sit back and wait. I wanted to be actively doing something. There is a fine line between trust and complacency. I felt like I owed it to Connor to arm myself with all of the information and possibilities for treatment available. In order for us to help Connor fight this insidious battle, we had to be fully prepared.

My first steps were to take inventory of what I could bring to the situation. My mom was a prayer warrior of quiet, faithful strength. I needed her to pray without ceasing. My father was a pastor. I knew I could call on him for biblical wisdom. My grandparents had instilled a great sense of eternal perspective within me. As I thought of these important people's influence on my life, one of my grandfather's favorite sayings came to mind: "This life on earth will soon be past; only what's done for Christ will last." Tait and I knew Jesus as Lord and Savior of our lives. We both believed in the absolute truth of God's Word. While we felt spiritually ready to fight for our son, we weren't sure what to do first. We decided to call every doctor we knew who could possibly advise us. Next, we scheduled a steady stream of family members to care for our other children. And finally, we prayed—a lot. With every waking breath, in every free moment in the day, we begged God to heal our son.

Initially we stayed in Dallas for Connor's treatments, since most hospitals follow the same initial protocol with pediatric cancer patients. But as Connor's situation became more complicated, we constantly found ourselves seeking new, cutting-edge treatments in hospitals throughout the country. It did not take long to realize that our son's ever-changing health needs would keep us in constant motion and in constant need of God's guidance.

Clinging to Prayer

Devote yourselves to prayer, being watchful and thankful.
—Colossians 4:2

Over the course of Connor's battle with neuroblastoma, we waited for hundreds—if not thousands—of test results. In the beginning, I agonized over each new test. But once I began praying before each test and thanking God in advance for His answer, I found myself becoming less anxious over time. The more I prayed and turned to God's Word, the more He showed me that He had an ultimate plan for Connor as well as perfect timing for everything in his life. Two verses in particular helped me to improve my prayer life And stay focused.

> My son, give attention to My words; incline your ears to My sayings. Do not let them depart from your eyes; keep them in the midst of your heart; for they are life to those who find them, and health to all their flesh. (Proverbs 4:20-22 NKJV) Consider it pure joy, my brothers, whenever you face trials of many kinds, because you know that the testing of your faith develops perseverance. Perseverance must finish its work so that you may be mature and complete, not lacking anything. (James 1:2-4 NIV)

Tait, Connor, and I experienced firsthand what happens when God's people pray. We saw miracles all along the way—bits of sunlight through the rain. We saw our family being taken care of during our darkest moments. We saw our son wrapped in God's loving arms. We saw Connor's ever-changing needs being met time and time again. We can honestly say that we experienced many blessings during this trial. Prayer was the igniting spark for all of these miracles. We were so blessed to have had an army of prayer warriors continually praying for our son.

Half-Full

> *Now faith is being sure of what we hope for and certain*
> *of what we do not see . . . without faith it is impossible to*
> *please God.*
> —Hebrews 11:1, 6

I have come to realize that, for the most part, the medical community tends to be cautious and often leans toward the negative side of reports and diagnoses. I understand that this is part of medical professionals' jobs—to help us realize the downside of medical problems and all the negative possibilities. But, I soon realized that for my sake and Connor's, I had to believe in the positive options available. My faith gave me courage to believe in unlikely possibilities and in the impossible—even in miracles. In her book, *Believing God*, Beth Moore explains why our faith is so important:

> We may as well accept faith challenges as a fact of life
> and not be shocked or feel picked on when they come.
> God brings them to build our faith, prove us genuine,
> and afford Himself endless excuses to reward us. He
> delights in nothing more than our choice to believe Him
> over what we see and feel.[1]

A nurse practitioner once asked us how we were able to "keep it together" during our whole ordeal. He commented that we seemed to just take everything in stride. I attributed our "togetherness" to two things. First, we have a great support team of friends and family members. We have so many people praying for us, and it has made such a huge difference. Second (and most importantly), our faith has sustained us. This was such a difficult situation to live through, and it would have been impossible without God. When we had moments of weakness or fear, we turned to Him and were blessed with His peace, comfort, and strength.

I Still Believe

> *Why are you downcast, O my soul? Why so disturbed within me? Put your hope in God, for I will yet praise Him, my Savior and my God.*
>
> —Psalm 43:5

Connor's prognosis was always unclear. We spent so many days and nights wondering, *Is his bone marrow clean? Is the disease in his bones dead? Are the inoperable tumors dead?* Every test brought answers and then more questions. We constantly had to trust God and to *believe* that the neuroblastoma was dead. When we could get no clear, definitive answers, we would send out mass prayer requests like the one below:

> Pray for answers to come soon. Pray for us to remember God's faithfulness. Pray for us to focus on the fact that He holds us in His loving arms. To me, this is just another test of our faith. I do not want to focus on my fears and anxieties. I want to focus on God. I still believe . . .

Is it naive to believe when no one else does? Is it foolish to have hope when doctors, friends, and "experts" tell you there is no chance of receiving the answer to your prayers? I don't think so. Tait remembers a special moment of hope he had with Connor during his first round of chemo:

> While waiting for Connor's chemo to drip on a summer day in 2005, we both looked out at the west and dreamed. We dreamed of going to Texas stadium and seeing the Cowboys play. I started telling him about the rock concerts I'd seen there. We talked about playing outside—running, laughing, chasing, and tumbling to the ground in exhaustion—a little boy in pajamas and a dad in shorts dreaming about baseball, bike rides, and fireworks.

When Connor's drip was done, and he was able to leave the tenth floor oncology area, we went down to the hospital lobby and out the front door. I carried him to a small twenty-by-twenty-foot patch of grass where the parking lot met the street. I cleared the trash and cigarettes, and we lay down in the grass. Our minds drifted to the rolling hills of Ireland and a sandy beach in Hawaii. We covered the globe on that day, and we stayed there until the moon came out and the stars put my son to bed. We dreamed big in the biggest backyard in the world that day.

Truth

I am the Lord your God, who teaches you what is best for
you, who directs you in the way you should go.
                                            —Isaiah 48:17

When you find yourself surrounded by people offering suggestions for what you should do, it is important to have a source of absolute truth. For my family, this truth can come only from the Word of God. We leaned on this truth constantly to comfort and guide us as we made each decision regarding Connor's treatment and path.

Following is a journal entry I wrote.

> Next Thursday, Connor will have a bone marrow biopsy to see if the cancer has come back in his bone marrow. This is just standard procedure. If the cancer is back, there is not a cure. I know that they are working on a cure for relapse with some experimental treatments. but nothing is proven yet. Pray that we can stand strong in our faith and not fear the outcome of this test. We are focusing on God and His Word (the voice of truth), and we believe that Connor is healed.

It is quite burdensome to have your child's "battle" be dependent on your decision for his next course of action. I realize God is in control, and He has directed our path in a most timely and remarkable manner, but we still want to make sure we are following His guidance for Connor. Do we continue to wait, or do we look for something more aggressive? Will something more aggressive tear Connor's strength down, leaving him unable to fight the cancer? Sometimes the weight of these questions is consuming. But Jesus gives this comfort: "Humble yourselves therefore under the mighty hand of God, that He may exalt you in due time; casting all your anxiety upon Him, because He careth for you" (1 Peter 5:6-7 KJV).

Of course we believe God has done, and will continue to do, great things through Connor's life. Connor has always been in God's hands, and He has always had a specific plan for his life. We continually seek His will, so that we can be assured that we are on the path He has designated for us to travel. Then we rest in His truth that because He cares for us, He will continue to guide us.

For Love

> *Love is patient, love is kind. It does not envy, it does not boast, it is not proud. It is not rude, it is not self-seeking, it is not easily angered, it keeps no record of wrongs. Love does not delight in evil but rejoices with the truth. It always protects, always trusts, always hopes, always perseveres. Love never fails.*
>
> —1 Corinthians 13:4-8a

Wow! That's a powerful verse, isn't it? Love *always* hopes, *always* perseveres. It *never* fails. What an outstanding promise, and here is another: "Perfect love casts out fear" (1 John 4:18).

A good friend of mine gave me a visual picture of this kind of love. He said, "If you were asked to walk across a wire three-hundred feet off the ground, would you do it for one million dollars?" My immediate response was no. I would be too afraid! Then my friend said, "What if your child was on that wire? Would you walk on the tight wire to save him?" Of course I would! Love is stronger than my fear. It *casts out* fear! Isn't that a beautiful example of what love can do?

I can relate to that example. My love for Connor compelled me to do *all* that was necessary for him. From the moment of his diagnosis, I was prepared to take my son anywhere, pay for any treatment, and fight for him until his last breath. But as much as I love Connor, I know God loves him more. He loves him so much more that He gave His life for Connor, which gives us the hope and perseverance to which we must cling. God promised to always take care of Connor and to provide a way for him (and us) to spend eternity in heaven. What a promise! What love!

Life Goes On

*For You created my inmost being; You knit me together in
my mother's womb. I praise You because I am fearfully and
wonderfully made; Your works are wonderful, I know that
full well.*
—Psalm 139:13-14

When we received Connor's initial diagnosis, I was five months
pregnant with our fourth child. Four months later, I gave birth to our
son Mason. Tait and I felt so blessed to hold a little new life in our
arms. This baby boy had gone through so much before he was even
born. I immediately knew that I had another tough little superhero
in my hands. I was so thankful for those who took the time to pray
for Connor and little Mason during my pregnancy. I know that God
heard these prayers and blessed us with a wonderful gift.

However, the excitement and hope of Mason's birth was quickly
tainted. While I was still in the hospital recovering, Tait had to
take Connor for another biopsy. During his last scan, the doctors
noticed something unusual in his nasal passages/cheek area.
Neuroblastoma can grow in the skull, so we had to investigate this
abnormality. *Could it possibly be a new cancer growth?* I didn't want
to consider that option. The hospital performed a CAT-scan-guided
needle biopsy. This was not the stress I wanted while Mason and I
were still in the hospital! I did not want our new baby's arrival to be
clouded with fear.

Thankfully, when we got the report back on Connor's
biopsy, there were no signs of "live" cancer. Either there
was no cancer there to begin with, or it was gone or dead
by then. God answered our prayers again. No matter
how scared or unsure Tait and I became, God was always
there. Through it all, He has always been faithful. "Let us
hold fast the confession of our hope without wavering,
for He who promised is faithful" (Hebrews 10:23).

The End of Pride

"For I know the plans for you," declares the Lord, "plans to prosper you and not to harm you, plans to give you hope and a future."

—Jeremiah 29:11

Following is a journal entry I wrote during Connor's second year of treatment. The treatment was a lot less strenuous and Connor was able to start playing some sports. It felt like a little bit of normalcy had come back into our lives.

Connor and Carson have started playing on a soccer team this fall. This is the first season for both of them. Connor has missed out on so much of the "sports scene" for the last year and a half. I can tell his energy level is not where it should be. He's also still rebuilding muscle tone from the muscle atrophy he developed from all of his time spent in a hospital bed during the transplants and surgery. It will take time for him to regain his strength and endurance. We are hoping that soccer and his karate classes will help with that.

As I watched Connor practice soccer last Saturday, I noticed how much better, quicker, and stronger the other children were. The other children were scoring goals and were quite skilled. I started feeling bad for Connor that he missed so much last year. While these other children were running and playing and developing strengths in soccer or whatever their sports were, Connor was fighting for his life in a hospital bed. I believe I was indulging in a little self-pity and envy. I shared my thoughts with Tait and said I wished I could see Connor score a goal or have his own "shining moment" on the field. Tait said (in his wisdom), "Just the fact that Connor is on the field today playing soccer, still with us, is his 'shining moment.'" How true! After all he's been through, he is able to run on a soccer field . . . although slower than the other kids. He's able to be part of a team like all the other kids . . . although he may not be the star player.

I suddenly saw the truth. My pride wanted Connor to be like the rest of the kids, able to excel at sports and receive recognition for his abilities. But then I realized Connor is excelling . . . just not by ways easily measured by onlookers. He excels in his perseverance, his determination, his bravery, and his joyful spirit in the midst of trial. Shame on me for trying to make him fit a mold—a mold that is easily seen and recognized by others. I will focus on the special qualities that God has given Connor, and I will cherish his uniqueness. God made Connor just the way He wanted him.

Chapter 3

In the Trenches

When your trial becomes normal and your struggle is day-to-day, you are in the trenches—the ugly part of the battle. Weary from fighting, you can barely lift your head out of the muddy waters that surround you. At this point, it can be difficult to see the big picture, namely because you are too busy extinguishing the incessant fires around you.

Watching a loved one struggle with any type of pain is particularly heart wrenching and exhausting. When Connor was very ill, I found myself decreasingly able to deal with my own emotions. Yet, I still had to find a way to get up each morning to take care of my son. The energy and strength it took to survive in these circumstances had to come from a supernatural source.

I've often heard it said that many people find God in foxholes. While that is true, I also know that many believers doubt God in the trenches. The Bible tells us that God wants us to bring our deepest needs, desires, and questions to Him in times of blessing and of trouble (1 Peter 5:7). Spending time in the trenches provides a unique opportunity to get to the core of our faith and beliefs. While your battle will be different from mine, I wanted to give you an idea of what our day-to-day struggles looked like during the worst part of Connor's illness. The *only* way I made it through these dark days was by keeping my focus on God. He is the ultimate source of strength.

There is no other way to make it through life's worst moments but to plug into His power source.

Here is a journal entry I wrote in the midst of my darkest days.

> Connor will start his first bone marrow transplant today. We are starting the most difficult part of our journey now. He will be in the hospital for approximately thirty days. This will be a challenge for our whole family. Baby Mason is three weeks old, and it will be so hard to be away from him. My mom and aunt will be helping out at home so that Tait and I can be at the hospital with Connor. Thankfully, close friends and family members will be helping us at the hospital as well. Some of them are even volunteering to spend the night with Connor (which he loves)! I know we will need God's supernatural strength to endure this. On the days that I sit with Connor in the clinic while he gets a blood or platelet transfusion, we are allowed to leave the clinic at 5 p.m. I always wonder how I can leave feeling so drained just from sitting all day. We will be facing a completely new level of exhaustion after spending the next month in the hospital. I pray that this emotional roller coaster I am on will level out. In the meantime, I know that we will need God's strength to get through every single moment of the next thirty days.

In Times of Frustration

> *Therefore you do not lack any spiritual gift as you eagerly*
> *wait for our Lord Jesus Christ to be revealed. He will keep*
> *you strong to the end, so that you will be blameless on the day*
> *of our Lord Jesus Christ.*
>
> —1 Corinthians 1:7-8

I think I've become an expert on frustration! After months without answers and days of not knowing exactly what to do next, frustration became a very familiar emotion. Yet, during my time in the trenches, I learned four great prayer-based survival tactics:

At the first sign of trouble, begin praying for supernatural peace. Pray for guidance in your encounters and as you access information. Ask for the Lord's direction to be made clear to you at exactly the right time.

Pray for quiet moments in your busy days so you can hear God speaking. During these times, ask God to confirm your choices multiple times so that you will know that He is indeed leading you.

Ask God to renew your hope and strength. In the midst of a long and arduous battle, you will become exhausted and will need times of rest and renewal.

Ask God to silence the Voice of the enemy from your thoughts. I always pray for resistance and enlightenment to the devil's schemes. I ask God to thwart the evil one's efforts to bring doubt and negativity to my mind. I then pray that glory would be brought to God's name through the manner in which I handle the trial.

Whether you are praying for a loved one who is ill or for a situation in your own life, thank God for the incredible resources He provides to help you through this period of frustration. Your prayer life can be a source of strength and peace. For me, my time in prayer was *the* time that I felt at peace and centered upon God. The chaos and fear that surrounded me would slip into the background of my mind as my conversation with God moved to the forefront. I clung to this time of peace in the midst of uncertainty.

Patience

Be strong and take heart, all you who hope in the Lord.
—Psalm 31:24

Following is a journal entry I wrote in the midst of his heavy treatment:

> Of course I would like for all of these treatments to be over, but God must have a reason for them to continue. There may be a family we need to meet and encourage or maybe there are other people we would not come in contact with if we were not still getting treatment. Whatever the reason, I am so glad that God is in control. I know He planned this whole journey for Connor even before he was born. Everything that happens is part of His plan. I find such comfort in knowing that God knows Connor intimately and that He is always watching over him. I can rest knowing that we will never be beyond God's reach.

It was always so hard for me to wait for test results. Patience has never been my strong suit, and spending hours sitting and waiting for what could be bad news was torturous. I just wanted to be finished with all the tests and all the nights spent in hospital rooms. I wanted to hit a magical fast-forward button that would whoosh us past all the painful treatments Connor had to endure. Yet, at the same time, I knew that God was working in me to strengthen my long-suffering abilities.

Frances J. Roberts had this to say about patience:

> "Be not weary in waiting for the Lord. Do not be disheartened if it seems to be delayed in coming. Lo, He is not slack concerning His promises. His times are not your times, and His patience endures forever. He can wait and not be anxious. While you see delay, He sees

His will being performed in ways not discernable to your
eye. What you see as standing still, He sees unfolding."[1]

How I wish I could see how God sees. Would I see that all
of this waiting is really just God's plan unfolding in His perfect
timing? I have to remind myself that God is working behind the
scenes—in a spiritual realm invisible to my human eyes. Despite
any circumstances I am facing or will face in the future, I can be
sure that God *is* working. I just have to work on avoiding weariness
as I wait.

Battle by Battle

> *He gives strength to the weary, and to him who lacks might*
> *He increases power.*
> —Isaiah 40:29

Following is a journal entry I wrote:

> Please pray for us as we prepare for another battle. I confess that Satan has been attacking us with fearful thoughts. He is trying to find our weakness. As we struggle against this battle in our minds, we continue to turn to God for strength, and He has not let us down. As I continue to get weaker and weaker, I feel His presence growing stronger and stronger. Satan may feel like he is gaining ground with us, but he has not and will not win this war. Christ has already won! At this point, we are laying Connor at His feet. God is on His throne; He is in control, not us, and He will never leave our side.

A few weeks ago, I gave my testimony in our Sunday school class. I mentioned that most of the time, I felt God's strength and peace during our journey. There were also many times when I felt weak and afraid. When Tait and I found ourselves praying for the strength to continue through another day, God never failed to reveal to us the incredible truths of His Holy Word. I know God is working on us as we go through this trial. "We rejoice in our sufferings, because we know that suffering produces perseverance; perseverance, character; and character, hope. And hope does not disappoint us, because God has poured out His love into our hearts by the Holy Spirit, whom He has given us" (Romans 5:3-5).

Although your journey may be dark and treacherous, God will always be there to guide you. When you seek Him earnestly in prayer, asking for His wisdom and guidance, He will not let you down. He will guide you one battle at a time. This is the only way to face a war of this magnitude—one battle at a time. You have to remain spiritually tenacious. I love this quote by Oswald Chambers: "Spiritual tenacity means to work deliberately on the certainty that God is not going to be worsted. One of the greatest strains in life is the strain of waiting for God. Remain spiritually tenacious."

Fighting the Good Fight

> *He delivered us from such a deadly peril, and He will deliver us. On Him we have set our hope that He will continue to deliver us, as you help us by your prayers. Then many will give thanks on our behalf for the gracious favor granted us in answer to the prayers of many.*
>
> —2 Corinthians 1:10-11

Following is a journal entry that Tait's sister, Christie, wrote:

Several weeks ago, I checked the connorcruse.com website. Often four to five hundred people check up on Connor in a single day! This is an amazing number of people praying, caring, loving Connor, and just wanting to share some of Tait and Joy's burden in a small way, if we can. Sometimes, all we hope for as Joy and Tait put one foot in front of the other is that they will hear the sounds of our footsteps walking with them. The funny thing is that Joy and Tait's faith, endurance, and wisdom are feeding us all as we try to help them. Every time we check in, we find Joy being . . . well . . . Joy. She is relentlessly courageous and faithful, trial after trial, disappointment after disappointment, finding God's hand in the smallest victory and sharing this with us.

Can you imagine the frustration Satan must feel about this family? He sends one of the most painful trials imaginable to a family, and with God's help, they turn it into a graduate-level course in faith for anyone who wants to tune in. If you were Satan, wouldn't you keep turning up the heat? Wouldn't you delight in the slightest sign of weariness, tension, or fear? Wouldn't you look for any weakness or place of entry so you could silence this message once and for all? "Shut up!" he must mutter to himself.

I often have this crazy wish for my little brother and his family. I wish we could chop this burden into a hundred tiny pieces and hand them out to all of us who would gladly take a few so they would not have such a heavy burden to carry on their own. Even though there are hundreds, if not thousands, of us walking the journey with Joy and Tait, it's not the same as living it, day after day, hour after hour.

It's taking a toll, folks. Satan has the heat at a high boil. The more intense the heat, the more intense our prayers must be. Joy and Tait are in the thick of it, in the trenches, and we need to climb down in there with them.

For the next several weeks, we need to bathe this family in constant prayer. When I walk in their house, I want to feel the Holy Spirit surrounding each of them with love and protection. I want to sense God's power and strength throughout the house. I want to look at each of their faces and see that they are glowing with renewal and inexplicable peace, feeling Christ every minute with them right there in their home.

Let's lift up Joy, Tait, and all their children in this season of hope as they fight the good fight. Thank you in advance from the bottom of my heart.

Depending on Him,
Christie

Waiting

> *Wait for the Lord; be strong and take heart and wait for the Lord.*
>
> —Psalm 27:14

Several times during Connor's illness, Tait and I found ourselves at a crossroad, needing to decide when and where to go for his next cancer treatment. Decisions were often slow and arduous. Conversations with doctors were always delayed. Plans got redirected. As much as I hate to admit it, waiting on God's plan to unfold was painstaking!

After twenty-eight months of treatment, I thought I would become immune to the frustrations of waiting. The majority of hours in my days were spent waiting: waiting to see a doctor, waiting to start a scan, waiting until the scan was over, waiting to get an infusion, etc. Tests that should have taken thirty minutes ended up taking three hours. Scans that should have started at 1:00 p.m. would begin at 4:00 p.m. Anyone who deals with hospitals regularly knows that this is to be expected. So now, when I find myself becoming impatient, I turn to God, the only One who can renew my spirit and my energy. I like this paragraph from Jim Cymbala's book *Fresh Faith*.

> Many of our struggles with faith have to do with timing. We believe, at least in theory, that God will keep His promises—but when? If the answer does not come as soon as we expect, fear begins to assault us, and then soon we are tempted to "throw away our confidence," ignoring the fact that "it will be richly rewarded" (Hebrews 10:35). Many times in life, God waits while a situation goes from bad to worse. He appears to let it slip over the edge, so that you and I say, "There's no way now for this to work out." But that is the point when the omnipotent God intervenes in our hopelessness and says, "Oh, really? Watch this . . . !" Sometimes, when we get into emergencies and the situation seems

totally hopeless—it's actually a setup. God wants to do something great. He wants to demonstrate His power, so that His name will be praised in a new and greater way.[2]

When You Are Weary

> *Come to Me, all who are weary and burdened, and I will give*
> *you rest. Take My yoke upon you and learn from Me, for I*
> *am gentle and humble in heart, and you will find rest for*
> *your souls. For My yoke is easy and My burden is light.*
>   —Matthew 11:28-30

Following is a journal entry I wrote:

> I have to admit that last week I was feeling weary in this
> long race, but then I discovered another wonderful truth.
> I was reminded that we have to lean solely on the Lord
> for our strength. Our own wellspring of strength often
> times comes up empty. So many times we want to give
> up because we feel overwhelmed and weak, but that is
> exactly where God steps in to hold us up if we will just
> rely fully on Him.

It is human nature for us to want to fix things, to be in control.
We believe that if we just work hard enough for something, it will
happen. In the midst of fighting for Connor, I quickly realized that
there was not much I could do in my own strength to fight this
beast called *cancer*. Sure, we tried to get the best treatments for
Connor, and we tried to keep him as healthy and happy as possible.
Ultimately, however, his outcome was in God's hands. At first, it was
difficult to rest in that promise. Initially, I had to surrender Connor
over to God every day and give up on my weak attempts to control
the situation or fix everything.

Looking back now, I realize that each time I tried to take the reins
back from God, I started to feel a heavy weight on my shoulders. I
felt so loaded down, because I couldn't do it all. In contrast, when
I was able to release control back to God, I felt immediate relief. I
actually felt lighter and free. What an incredible blessing to feel our
burdens removed by the One who is capable of carrying the weight
of the world.

Fear

He will have no fear of bad news; his heart is steadfast, trusting in the Lord.
—Psalm 112:7

Fear is a strong emotion. It can render you speechless. It can make a grown man cry. It can immobilize you. It can consume your thoughts. Fear can make you nauseated. It can steal sleep from the tired and weary. It can alter your perception of reality. Fear can control your world, if you let it.

As we walked through our daily fight with cancer, fears taunted us from every angle: *Will Connor make it through the surgery? Will the surgeon get the entire tumor? How will the next scan or report look?* It was hard to keep these thoughts at bay while I was sitting alone in the waiting room (sometimes all day) waiting to speak with a doctor. By the time I would see the doctor, the ball in the pit of my stomach would have doubled in size. Then, I would have to put on a happy face for Connor. I couldn't let him see the fear as it crossed my face. I've come to realize that fear and faith cannot reside in the same place. If my faith increases, it will push out the fear. It will be a slow process, but leaning on Him is the best way to start. In moments like these, I imagined myself drowning in a raging sea, raising my arms to the only One who could save me. Once saved, I would cling to His precious promises:

> For the Spirit God gave us does not make us timid, but gives us power, love and self-discipline. 2 Timothy 1:7

> The Lord is my light and my salvation—whom shall I fear? The Lord is the stronghold of my life—of whom shall I be afraid? (Psalm 27:1)

> Fear not, for I have redeemed you; I have summoned you by name, you are Mine. When you pass through the waters, I will be with you; and when you pass through

the rivers, they will not sweep over you. When you walk through the fire, you will not be burned, the flames will not set you ablaze. For I am the Lord, your God, the Holy One of Israel, your Savior. (Isaiah 43:1-3)

Peace I leave with you; my peace I give you. I do not give to you as the world gives. Do not let your hearts be troubled and do not be afraid. (John 14:27)

So do not fear, for I am with you; do not be dismayed, for I am your God. I will strengthen you and help you; I will uphold you with My righteous right hand. (Isaiah 41:10)

Moving Mountains

For I know that through your prayers and the help given by
the Spirit of Jesus Christ, what has happened to me will turn
out for my deliverance.
—Philippians 1:19

Following is a journal entry I wrote to those who followed our blog, so they could keep updated on Connor's progress and pray for him:

This verse reminds me of a praise/worship song that says, "The prayers of a righteous one can move mountains, and I need a mountain moved. I need a mountain moved." Your words are so encouraging to us, and they help us realize that we are not alone in our prayers for Connor. Tait and I know God is hearing your prayers to give us all strength, because we feel His strength, peace, joy, and comfort every day. Tait said he feels like we are pushing this bus with Connor in it, and as we look closely at the bus, there are fingerprints all over it. The fingerprints are all of you helping us push this bus with the power of prayer. God is hearing our prayers and speeding this "bus" right along.

Because of your prayers, God's love and compassion continue to rain down on us daily. We know that even if "mountains are shaken and hills are removed, God's unfailing Love will not be shaken." (Isaiah 54:10) His love has become so real to us during these trying times. I am so glad that our Lord's love is so great and knows no end.

Purpose in Pain

> *I raised you up for this very purpose, that I might display*
> *My power in you and that My name might be proclaimed in*
> *all the earth.*
>
> —Romans 9:17

Jesus talked about having purpose in our suffering. He answered the disciples' question about why a man was born blind by saying, "Neither this man nor his parents sinned," said Jesus, "but this happened so that the works of God might be displayed in him." (John 9:3)

When we kneel expectantly before God to ask for healing, success, and rescue from our pain, we envision the perfect answer to our prayers. I constantly prayed for God's power to be displayed in my son's life through healing. That sounded like a great plan to me—Connor's cancer would disappear and God would be glorified. After all, God's power is obvious when relationships are restored, efforts are rewarded, and bodies are healed. But is God's glory diminished for those of us who don't get our miracle? Perhaps not.

Whatever Connor's outcome, our miracle is that God has given us a spirit of acceptance and even joy in the midst of a tremendous trial. Hope and peace beyond our understanding are evidence of God's power working in us. I love the way Nancy Guthrie explains it in her book *Hearing Jesus Speak into Your Sorrow*:

> "To experience and exude peace when life is crashing
> down around you, to have the lightness of joy when the
> weight of sorrow is heavy, to be grateful for what God
> has given you when you've lost what is most precious to
> you—that is God at work on the interior of your life, on
> display in your life."

In the midst of our trial, I know that God has a purpose in our pain. Our pain will have meaning as others see how being connected to God can be the only source of joy and hope in such a difficult time as this. We want to know that there is some meaning and purpose in our pain—that it is not random and worthless. We want to see how God is using our loss for good. That is where our faith is so important—faith that God is working out all things for the good of those who love Him, faith that the day will come when what we can't see now will become clear, and faith that He will give us the grace to get through this. "And we know that in all things God works for the good of those who love him, who have been called according to his purpose" (Romans 8.28).

Connor and I in Hawaii, March 2009.
Photo by Lisa Hoang.

Four generations: MacKenzie Cruse (daughter), Joyce Vilhauer (Maternal Grandmother), Zilpha Mann (Maternal Great-Grandmother), Joy Cruse (mother) and Connor Cruse, February 2001, on Connor's Baby Dedication Day. Photo by Tait Cruse.

Connor and big sister MacKenzie, ride a battery-powered motorcycle,
Sumer 2002. Photo by Joy Cruse.

Connor and BFF Mollie-Claire Matthews, Halloween 2003,
photo by Joy Cruse.

Christmas morning 2004, less than five months before Connor's
neuroblastoma diagnosis. Carson was 3, Connor 4 and MacKenzie 7.
Photo by Joy Cruse.

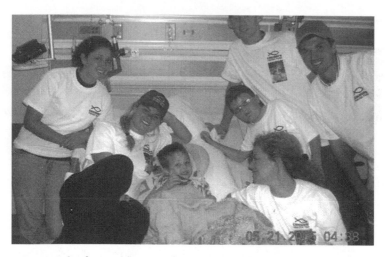

First week of neuroblastoma diagnosis at Children's Medical Center
Dallas, May 2005. Left to right: Christina Hampton, Lexie Warrick Allen
(cousin), Connor, (Aunt) Christie Warrick, Ryan Roach, Keith Roach and
Mitch Warrick (cousin). Photo by Joy Cruse.

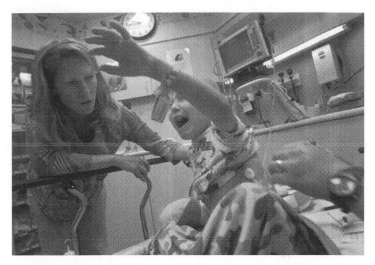

Connor screams in pain while I try to comfort him: as a nurse hooks him
up for a blood transfusion at Children's Medical Center Dallas. June 2005.
Photo by Rick Gershon.

Connor, Summer 2005. Photo courtesy of Children's
Medical Center Dallas.

MacKenzie, Carson, Connor and Tait on the Gator at Grandpa Vilhauer's farm in Stigler, Oklahoma, while taking a break between hospital stays, Fall 2005.

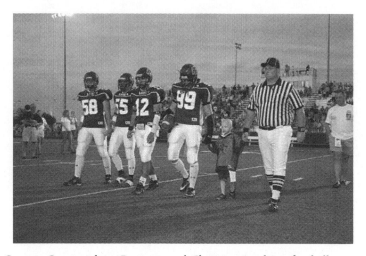

Connor Cruse night at Prestonwood Christian Academy football game. Fall 2005. Childhood cancer survivor and team captain Tim Flores is number 99. He orchestrated Connor Cruse night along with PCA Coach Mike Hall to encourage Connor. Photo by Manny Flores.

Ground breaking ceremony for Children's Medical Center—Legacy in Plano, Texas. November 2005, right before Connor's first bone marrow transplant. Photo courtesy of Children's Medical Center Dallas.

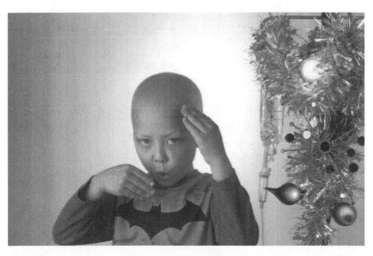

Kung Fu Connor fights cancer, Christmas 2005. Photo courtesy of Children's Medical Center Dallas.

Connor's lemonade stand at Stonebriar Country Club, Frisco, Texas, for the Chip Moody Golf Tournament benefiting Children's Medical Center Dallas. June 2006. Photo by Joy Cruse.

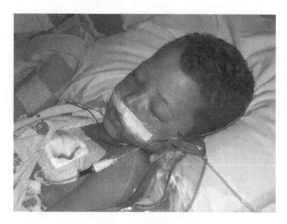

Connor in ICU at Children's Hospital in Boston, July 2006, after surgery to remove the primary tumor. The surgeon could only remove 70% of it. Photo by Rick Gershon.

The Cruse family (left-to right) Tait, Carson, Connor, Mason, Joy and MacKenzie, September 2006. Photo by Tom Warrick.

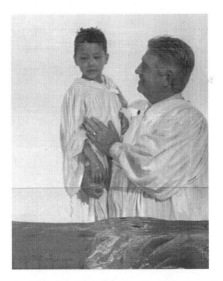

Prestonwood Baptist Church Senior Pastor Jack Graham baptized Connor December, 2006. Photo courtesy of Prestonwood Baptist Church.

Connor on New Hampton Beach, CT—after the Reach The Beach Relay, Summer '07. Photo by Tait Cruse.

Connor and Carson playing in our backyard. They were inseparable. They loved playing in the back yard with sticks, balls, nerf guns and light sabers. Summer 2007. Photo by Tait Cruse.

Tait and Connor swimming in our pool, Summer 2007.

Grandma Joyce Vilhauer and Connor in Playa Del Carmen, Mexico.
Family vacation, August 2007. Photo by Joy Cruse.

Connor and Mason play together on the beach in Playa del Carmen,
Mexico, August 2007. Photo by Joy Cruse.

Connor, Fall 2007. Photo by Catherine Clay.

Connor Cruse, Fall 2007. Photo by Catherine Clay.

Joy, Carson and Connor . . . the three amigo's . . . doing some serious battle in the backyard, Summer 2008. Photo by Tait Cruse.

Mason, Carson and Connor with Sayers Collins at Grandpa Vilhauer's
farm in Stigler, Oklahoma. Spring Break, 2009.
Photo by Joy Cruse.

Connor peers over his dad's shoulder at Glen Eagles Country club in
Plano, TX for the III Forks Golf Classic benefiting TeamConnor. April
2009. Photo by David Alvey.

Connor, just hours after being released from Children's Medical
Center—Legacy, June 2009, one month before he lost his four-year battle
with cancer. Photo by David Alvey.

Chapter 4

Putting on Armor

When you realize that your particular battle is increasing in length and intensity, it is time to face reality: you can't do this alone. Even with well-intentioned friends and doctors encouraging you to "keep going" and "keep fighting," you will undoubtedly reach a point of exhaustion and vulnerability.

So where do you turn? Who or what will protect you from the mental strain, the emotional highs and lows, and the physical toll that a life-changing struggle brings? My husband has a saying that he likes to repeat: "In difficult times, people will turn to the bed, the bottle, or the Bible." I hate to admit it, but he's probably right. The world offers its acceptable forms of escape from pain: alcohol, drugs, and denial. Each of these options comes with lasting consequences and no real resolution. But the Bible offers the free gift of wisdom, freedom, and eternal life through Jesus Christ. This reminds me of an often forgotten fact in a well-known story. In 1 Samuel 17, a shepherd boy named David steps up to fight the dreaded Goliath. King Saul approaches the boy and offers to gird him with his royal armor. Verse 39 gives us David's response to being fitted with Saul's protective covering: "'I cannot go in these,' he said to Saul, 'because I am not used to them.' So he took them off." David did not need this type of physical protection, and he knew it. He had all the security he needed via the mighty hand of God.

The protection God offers to each of us is spiritual and powerful. It guards us against the Devil's fiery arrows and evil schemes. If we are going to survive life's trials, we must be properly armed. Our efforts to protect ourselves will always fall short since we do not battle against flesh and blood (Ephesians 6:12). Connor's battle with cancer was continuous for four years. Sometimes the battle was intense and arduous, filled with surgeries, chemotherapy, radiation treatments, and bone marrow transplants. Other times we were trapped in holding patterns, temporarily removed from the heated fight as we waited to see how Connor's body would respond to the treatments he had received.

Any time you find yourself under attack, realize that Satan is close at hand ready to whisper lies, insert doubts, and implement his best game plan. This is nothing new—the evil one's schemes began in the garden of Eden when he lured Eve into a line of thinking that would cause her to doubt the only source of love and security she knew. Her pride got the best of her as she toyed with the idea of "becoming like God." *Perhaps she didn't really need God . . .* thus began her crisis of faith.

The Bible tells us that we should not be surprised when we encounter trials (1 Peter 4:12-13). Instead, we should be prepared. "Finally, be strong in the Lord and in his mighty power. Put on the full armor of God so that you can take your stand against the devil's schemes. For our struggle is not against flesh and blood, but against the rulers, against the authorities, against the powers of this dark world and against the spiritual forces of evil in the heavenly realms" (Ephesians 6:10-12). The story of David's defeat of Goliath is an excellent example of trusting in the Lord instead of focusing on our fears. I often told Connor that he reminded me of David. He was a young boy facing his own giant—cancer. Just as God helped David conquer Goliath, God sent His Son Jesus to conquer death for Connor (and for all those who believe).

I know it would have been easy for David to focus on his fear when he faced Goliath, but he chose to believe God's promises. God promised that He would protect David and give him victory. David told Goliath, "You come against me with sword and spear and javelin, but I come against you in the name of the Lord Almighty, the God of the armies of Israel, whom you have defied. This day the Lord will deliver you into my hand" (1 Samuel 17:45-46).

Those are not words of fear. They are words of faith. Just like David, I want to clothe myself daily with the armor of God and His voice of truth.

Inexplicable Peace

And the peace that passes all understanding will guard your
hearts and your minds in Christ Jesus.
—Philippians 4:7

Recently I have been thinking about all the different names for God, such as Prince of Peace, Lamb of God, and King of Kings. I've always known these names, but during Connor's illness I experienced their true meaning.

One name that gave me great comfort was Prince of Peace. "For to us a Child is born, to us a Son is given, and the government will be on His shoulders. And He will be called Wonderful Counselor, Mighty God, Everlasting Father, Prince of Peace" (Isaiah 9:6).

There is a verse that I love to read that gives me peace when I feel afraid or troubled. "Peace I leave with you, MY PEACE I give you. I do not give to you as the world gives. Do not let your hearts be troubled and do not be afraid" (John 14:27). It is so true that God gives us peace that this world cannot give. I'm so glad I'm plugged into a God who gives me His wonderful peace.

Over the last four years, hundreds of people have asked me, "How do you do it? How can you cope with your situation?" My answer is always the same: God gave me His peace when I could not find it in the doctors' answer or when I feared for Connor's future. He gave me His peace when I saw suffering on Connor's face or when Connor missed his family during a hospital stay. God gave me His peace when our younger son, Carson, asked, "When is Connor coming home?" Thank God for His peace "that passes all understanding." Granted there were many moments when I felt afraid, but overall, it was inexplicable peace that I felt.

We all want peace in life, but it can be so hard to find. Our busy, hectic schedules are not conducive to peace. Many people search their whole lives for peace but are looking in the wrong places. They try to find it through meditation, yoga, tranquility, knowledge, or medication. They try changing their outward circumstances and hope to discover it in others' approval. Through this whole journey with Connor, I have found that there is only one true source of peace for me . . . Jesus.

Strength

> *God is our refuge and strength, a very present help in trouble.*
>
> —Psalm 46:1

I heard a wonderful sermon on strength from our pastor, Jack Graham. He said, "All Christians will face difficulties and struggles. But there is one element that separates those who live a defeated life from those who live a victorious life. It all has to do with where you find your source of strength."[1]

The source of your strength—I had to stop and think about that. From whom or what was I drawing my strength? I must admit that sometimes I gather my strength from knowledge. Many times I convinced myself that if I surf the Internet long enough and find all the best doctors and treatments, I would find the ability to defeat my son's cancer. Other times I pulled strength from my abilities. I have a strong will and a deep desire to fight for my children. Again I told myself that if I kept fighting I would eventually "win."

Now I realize that knowledge and personal strength are both limited. Only in God's strength can we truly find victory. Perhaps you are facing problems with your health, family, finances, or career. Whatever you are facing, look to the Lord for His strength. Even if it seems like you will never come out from under the weight of despair, when you wait upon God and draw strength from His Word and His presence, He will give you the strength you need to persevere.

Be encouraged today by the words of Isaiah 40:29-31: "He gives power to the faint, and to him who has no might He increases strength. Even youths shall faint and be weary, and young men shall fall exhausted; but they who wait for the Lord shall renew their strength; they shall mount up with wings like eagles; they shall run and not be weary; they shall walk and not faint." The Lord knows your situation, and He is with you to help you through this time. When you feel that all of your strength is gone, invite the Lord to renew you with His strength.

Faithfulness

Be strong and courageous. Do not be frightened, and do not
be dismayed, for the Lord your God is with you wherever you
go.—Joshua 1:9

I've been studying the Israelites' journey to the Promised Land in my Bible study class. It's amazing how many times that, even though they were being guided by God's visible presence, they became frightened and discouraged. From my vantage point, I think I understand their emotions. Because they could not see their destination, they began to forget from where they had come. They forgot their years of enslavement. They forgot the death, plagues, and destruction behind them. They only saw their present state of frustration.

So what did God do to encourage His children? He reminded them of how far He had taken them. "Only be careful, and watch yourselves closely so that you do not forget the things your eyes have seen or let them fade from your heart as long as you live. Teach them to your children and to their children after them. (Deuteronomy 4:9).

God warns His children that if they forget His faithfulness, His Red Sea miracle, their hearts might wander—which did happen on numerous occasions. "and they did not remember the LORD their God, who had rescued them from the hands of all their enemies on every side". (Judges 8:34)

Following is a journal entry I wrote when Connor was in the hospital for his second bone marrow transplant. He was very sick with a bacterial infection. This was very dangerous for him, because he had no white blood cells due to the strength of the chemotherapy he received during his transplant. This means that he had no immune system and no way to even fight the common cold, or this infection. Slowly, his white blood count increased and he was able to overcome the infection.

I am praying that I will follow God's instructions. I do not want to forget how far He has brought Connor, how far he has carried our family. Connor is our Red Sea miracle. This remembrance will help me focus on His faithfulness when new trials arise. It will remind me that He will never leave me nor forsake me, just as God reminded Joshua as he prepared to lead the Israelites into their Promised Land. More great news . . . the doctor came in this morning and said yesterday's blood culture showed no signs of a bacterial infection. Praise God again! *God is so good!* We will be forever grateful for the prayers of so many.

Helping Hands

> As long as Moses held up his hands, the Israelites were
> winning, but whenever he lowered his hands, the Amalekites
> were winning. When Moses' hands grew tired, they took a
> stone and put it under him and he sat on it. Aaron and Hur
> held his hands up—one on one side, one on the other—so that
> his hands remained steady till sunset. So Joshua overcame the
> Amalekite army with the sword.
>
> —Exodus 17:11-30

Following is a journal entry I wrote during Connor's bone marrow
transplant when we relied on so many friends and family members
for support, love and prayers:

> Tait and I feel like Moses. We need to continually
> hold up God in our lives so Connor can focus on God
> and overcome the cancer. All of you are Aaron and
> Hur—helping us and supporting us so we can glorify
> God for Connor and others to see. It is not an easy job,
> and that is why we need your help as Moses needed Aaron
> and Hur. It is too hard to walk this journey alone.

In Romans 12, Paul compares the members of the body of Christ
to the individual parts of the human body—each having a specific
function and purpose. Being in a position of need allowed me to
experience firsthand how and why God established His church to
function in this special way.

I can't count the number of times that Tait and I found ourselves
in need of help in some way. We constantly needed someone to watch
our other children, take them to school, and make sure their needs
were being met at home. Connor needed tutoring for the school
days he missed during and after his surgeries and treatments. Tait
needed help preparing meals and tackling the mounds of laundry
that accumulated while I spent night after night in the hospital with
Connor. God provided for each and every need we encountered

by sending gifted, patient, and generous people who were eager to use their God-given gifts. Connor's teacher came to tutor him as he sat through blood transfusions. My niece joyfully picked up our children from school and made sure their homework was done each night. And a group of ladies from our Sunday school class came to do our laundry!

These acts of service strengthened our faith and lifted our spirits. Through the gifts of time and service from fellow believers, God continued to pour out His love, compassion, and mercy upon our family.

Standing in the Gap

Finally, my brethren, be strong in the Lord and in the power of His might. Put on the whole armor of God, that you may be able to stand against the wiles of the devil. For we do not wrestle against flesh and blood, but against principalities, against powers, against the rulers of the darkness of this age, against spiritual hosts of wickedness in the heavenly places. Therefore take up the whole armor of God, that you may be able to withstand in the evil day, and having done all, to stand.

—Ephesians 6:10

Following is a journal entry I wrote after Connor had completed his standard protocol of treatment for neuroblastoma:

While we do not have remission, we have Connor with us to enjoy and watch grow. There's no explanation for the bizarre state of his cancer. We are becoming accustomed to his new state of disease—stable refractory neuroblastoma. It is residual, but thank God it is stable and not growing. He still has cancer, but he is essentially thriving. I sometimes wonder if there is a daily battle going on in Connor at a microscopic level. Are there entire armies fighting, one evil (cancer cells) and one good (his body's defenses, armed with chemotherapy and led by the hand of God), every day, every hour, every minute?

And if that's the case, what role has prayer played in this? How many of you have supported the troops in Connor's little body by lifting him up and calling on the Lord daily for this battle where his life hangs in the balance? I realize that there are likely thousands of people praying hundreds and hundreds of prayers. There is no way to express the awe I feel at the thought of so many people praying for Connor day after day.

I also often wonder what will become of a young boy who has been prayed for so much. What effect do thousands of prayers for one person have on that person besides keeping him alive? I cannot help but think he is being prepared for something special in God's plan.

In summary, I want to humbly thank all of you for standing in the gap, day after day. And to say I hope you will continue so we all can see what God has in store for Connor. Don't let up!

Unfailing Love

But the eyes of the Lord are on those who fear Him, on those whose hope is in His unfailing love.

—Psalm 33:18

It was always scary when I had those difficult conversations with Connor's doctors. They were concerned about Connor's precarious situation. During those times, it was so easy to start thinking of all the negative possibilities. I think the doctors always felt it was necessary to share all of the possible bad and terrifying scenarios, and their words would never ensure my comfort or peace. I would have to remind myself that God was worthy to be trusted. He would provide a way, a path for our shaky steps and our tender hearts. I know that God has never lost control even when life doesn't make sense. This is where I really need to trust Him and remember that He is always near.

As I reread many of my journal entries in preparation for this book, I found myself overwhelmed by God's incessant attention to our needs, down to the smallest detail. At many of these crossroads, we were at a loss for direction and for more options, but God always provided a path for us. Thank you, Lord, for guiding our steps and providing us with what we needed when we needed it.

Joy Cruse

Sufficiency

> But he said to me, "My grace is sufficient for you, for my power is made perfect in weakness." Therefore I will boast all the more gladly about my weaknesses, so that Christ's power may rest on me.
>
> —2 Corinthians 12:9

I've often heard the phrase, "the great I AM" in reference to God, but recently it has had a deeper meaning for me. I realize that God *is* whatever we need Him to be at any specific moment. That's why He is the great I AM. You can finish the phrase "I am . . ." with anything holy, and God can be that for you. It's like a fill-in-the-blank game. He didn't put a word after "I AM," because we can finish the sentence however we need to.

For those who have lost a loved one, He can be your Comforter. For those who need guidance, He can be your Counselor. If you need healing, He is the Great Physician. He can be your strength when you are weak and He can be peace in your turmoil. He is whatever we need Him to be!

Boldness

Now to Him who is able to do immeasurably more than all
we ask or imagine, according to His power that is at work
within us.

—Ephesians 3:20

Following is a journal entry I wrote during the time of low dose treatment for Connor. This period in our lives felt like we were experiencing some normalcy again:

At the end of each school year, the teachers at Connor's school hand out certificates to each of their students indicating each student's strongest character trait. Connor's trait was *enthusiasm*, which means, "expressing with my spirit the joy of my soul." His teacher referenced the verse "Rejoice always . . . Do not quench the spirit" (1 Thessalonians 5:16, 19).

At camp last summer, the counselors said his character trait was boldness. When I picked Connor up every day after Sky Ranch's day camp, he would tell me how great it was and ask if he could come back next year. He was so enthusiastic.

I think both words exemplify Connor's character. He approaches life with such enthusiasm and boldness. Whether it is the way he loves with such exuberance or the way he approaches his fight against cancer with tenacity and silent perseverance, I am amazed! The past three years of this intense battle have not quenched his spirit. It is just more evidence of God's hand on his life. I see now that God has strengthened my son for this battle. As a toddler, he was very whiny and clingy when he didn't feel well. Now, he treats feeling ill as a passing annoyance. I picked him up from baseball camp yesterday and asked him how it went. He said his favorite part was batting and his least favorite was running around the

71

field. He told me how he'd gotten half way around the field when he started coughing uncontrollably until he vomited. He then took a deep breath and completed the lap. No big deal. As I said earlier, God has given Connor strength and fortitude beyond his seven years to endure this battle.

I'll leave you with this prayer from Stormy Omartian's *Power of a Praying Parent*. I think the words are beautiful and relevant to our situation.

"Lord, You alone know the depth of the burden we carry. We may not understand the specifics, but you have measured the weight of it on our shoulders. I don't want to minimize what You are doing in our lives, for I know You work great things in the midst of trials."[3]

The Praise on My Lips

I will extol the Lord at all times; His praise will always be on my lips. My soul will boast in the Lord; let the afflicted hear and rejoice. Glorify the Lord with me; let us exalt His name together. I sought the Lord, and He answered me; He delivered me from all my fears.

—Psalm 34:1-4

I've never considered praise to be a weapon. But the Bible gives us the account of Paul and Silas in prison to support this claim. As they sang praises to God, the chains that bound them fell to the ground. Symbolically, the chains that bind us will fall when we praise God—chains such as worry, defeat, and fear will release their hold on us.

When things are running smoothly, praise comes easily to our lips. But as I look back over the last thirty months, I can't say that praise was easy very often. Sometimes Tait and I felt we were in a pit of despair. In those times, extolling the Lord was much more challenging; it was a bigger test of faith. As we reached Connor's eighth birthday, our hearts turned to gratefulness and praise!

Following is a journal entry that Tait wrote:

> It has been 1,216 days since Connor was diagnosed on May 15, 2005. Today, October 2, 2008, we celebrate his birthday. Connor is eight years old. My son is eight years old! My son has walked this journey for 1,216 days, and oh, how grateful we are for his being eight. How grateful we are for Legos™ on the carpet when we step on them in the middle of the night. How grateful we are for his fun-loving, adventurous spirit. How grateful we are for 1,216 days of life!
>
> Thank you, my friends, for your prayers and support. Tonight, while you are getting ready for bed, please say a little prayer, and thank God that Connor is eight years old.

I like the words from Frances J. Roberts' *On the Highroad of Surrender*. "You will find courage in the hour of calamity if you have disciplined your spirit to rest always in the Lord and to praise continually regardless of circumstances. Any lesser plane of thinking is not only disquieting to the soul but will also open the door to a host of sins. Anger, resentment, petulance, bitterness—none of which can live in an atmosphere of praise—will thrive if the eyes of the soul are diverted to the natural situation and are not fixed on Christ."[4]

I just love that. It reminds me to keep my eyes fixed on Him in all circumstances and to continuously praise Him.

Chapter 5

Winning and Losing

Throughout Connor's battle with cancer, our family faced many challenges to our faith. We quickly learned that, even when we are armed for battled, we are not guaranteed the specific "win" for which we pray. Faith is a journey, not a one-time decision. We must wake up each day and ask to be guided by God's Holy Spirit. And then we must trust completely in His guidance.

But that doesn't mean that we can't bring our disappointment to God. As a loving, attentive heavenly Father, He desires our honest communication with Him. So when you look around and see the prayers of others answered and not your own, it is okay to cry out to Him. Psalm 56:8 says of God, "You keep track of all my sorrows. You have collected all my tears in Your bottle. You have recorded each one in Your book." That is how aware God is of the state of your heart and emotions. He keeps track of every tear!

In the fight against cancer, many battles are won and lost. Each step forward seems to be followed by two steps back. After Connor's initial high-intensity treatment, we flew to Boston for a tumor resection led by Dr. Shamberger, a specialist in the area of neuroblastoma surgery. We faced the procedure with high hopes that this competent surgeon could remove the entire primary tumor in Connor's abdomen.

Our hopes were dashed when the surgeon emerged from the operating room saying he could only reach 70 percent of the tumor. The remaining 30 percent was inoperable. Trying to stay positive, we held on to the hope that the remaining tumor was dead or necrotic. Based on what the surgeon saw, he felt the tumor looked necrotic. We would just have to wait on the pathology results.

The initial results were outstanding. The tumor appeared to be dead. Yet our celebration was short-lived, as the final test results were unclear. Some of the cells were questionable. With neuroblastoma, if there is any question, you must continue the fight (and the treatment).

Our next step in Connor's treatment took us to New York, where he was offered a specialized treatment for refractory (residual) neuroblastoma. After his first scan in New York, the doctors informed us that the cancer in Connor's bones was still alive. This news came six months after his primary doctors had declared his bones to be cancer free. It all boiled down to the way the radiologists interpreted the scans. Another defeat and another step backward.

You can imagine the frustration and the overwhelming confusion we felt. Welcome to the dance called cancer.

These are just a couple of examples of our losses on the battlefield. There is nothing harder than getting back up and continuing the fight after a devastating defeat. But these times made us realize just how tightly we had to hold on to our support groups, our war chest, our armor, and our God.

Looking for Signs

Remember Your word to Your servant, for You have given me hope. My comfort in my suffering is this; Your promise preserves my life.

—Psalm 119:49-50

Following is a journal entry that I wrote after Connor's initial protocol of treatment was over. At this point, Connor was seeking treatment in New York:

> So our trip to New York did not turn out the way we had expected. Because Connor still had active cancer in his bones, he would not be able to participate in this particular hospital's specialized treatment program. Instead, he would start a new type of outpatient chemotherapy. Connor's kindergarten year just got more difficult. In addition, our doctors are giving us mixed recommendations on whether or not we should expect the chemo to work.
>
> This momentary defeat will not keep us down. We will get back up and continue to fight. The only difference is the fight just got longer. I just wish I could see the finish line.

Shortly after this journal entry, I mentioned to my mom that it would be so nice to have some evidence from God, such as a letter that said Connor would eventually be healed. The letter could even say that this journey will take longer than expected but that he will be healed in the end. Then, the road to the finish line would be long, but it would be much easier to manage. My mom then read me these words from Joni Eareckson Tada, from her book, *Pearls of Great Price.*

> We say to God, "If you don't mind, please show me where I am going. I don't need to see the whole road, but at

least a little bit." We think our faith has to be supported by a bit of evidence. A hint, a signpost, a whisper . . . something to give us a clue as to what God is doing. We wrongly assume that faith is the ability to take a couple of puzzle pieces and be able to envision the entire picture. Not so. Faith that must be supported by the five senses is not genuine. Jesus said to doubting Thomas, "You have believed me because you have seen Me, but blessed are those who have not seen and yet believe."[1]

Healing Power

*He heals the brokenhearted and binds up their wounds.
He determines the number of the stars and calls them
each by name. Great is our Lord and mighty in power; His
understanding has no limit.*

—Psalm 147:3-5

Following is a journal entry I wrote:

After Connor finished two rounds of the outpatient
chemo that targeted his bone disease, we received the
scan results . . . hallelujah! The final report confirmed
the preliminary report! This is truly a miracle. In most
cases, when a child with neuroblastoma goes through the
double transplant and still has some "refractory" disease,
the cancer has become resistant to the chemotherapy.
Because of Connor's status, some doctors warned me that
it would not be surprising if Connor did not respond at
all to the chemotherapy. The best-case scenario that I was
given was that he might improve, but not by a lot. That's
why we were praying for the scans to show the disease
in the bones to be clear. Now there is no doubt (to us,
anyway) that God took control and cleaned up his bones
from the cancer. Connor responded to the chemo way
beyond anyone's expectations (except ours). Praise God
for His healing power! We are ecstatic here in the Cruse
household! I heard the song "Indescribable" by Chris
Tomlin today. What a perfect expression of praise to our
God who is worthy!

Perseverance

> *Therefore, since we are surrounded by so great a cloud of witnesses, let us also lay aside every weight, and sin which clings so closely, and let us run with endurance the race that is set before us, looking to Jesus, the founder and perfecter of our faith.*
>
> —Hebrews 12:1

Following is a journal entry I wrote:

After we received the news that Connor's bone disease was clear, we flew back to New York for a re-scan that would hopefully qualify us for the specialized treatment. Their results, again, were different from the ones we received in Dallas. But all the doctors agreed that the disease in his bones did lessen considerably. Praise God for that.

However, the doctors were not willing to declare that his bones were clear. Therefore, we have been sent home once again to continue with more of the same outpatient chemo.

I have to admit that it is hard to wrap my mind around this latest development. I feel weary, frustrated, and impatient. It is frustrating to continue this course of more chemo. I feel like each time we get close to the finish line, the line keeps getting pushed farther out. But, as the shock wears off, I know we will rally again and step back into the ring—or the race. We're ready to fight once more. I just need to remember that God will help us get to the finish line, whenever and wherever it is. These words from Beth Moore's Bible study, *Believing God*, help me persevere.

"If the primary objective is to show His supremacy, perhaps He might choose to heal instantaneously. If His primary objective is to teach sufficiency in Him or to mature and build faith, I wonder whether He heals through a process or stich-by-stich method. Remember, God is far more interested in our knowing the Healer than He is in the healing. God can be vastly glorified through either objective: showing His supremacy or His sufficiency."[2]

I guess where Connor is concerned, God is showing us His sufficiency. So, we will continue to fully rely on Him.

Blessings in Unanswered Prayers

> *Praise be to the God and Father of our Lord Jesus Christ,*
> *the Father of compassion and the God of all comfort, who*
> *comforts us in all our troubles, so that we can comfort those*
> *in any trouble with the comfort we ourselves have received*
> *from God.*
>
> —2 Corinthians 1:3-4

After Connor's initial diagnosis, we spent forty-five days hoping and praying that the cancer would miraculously disappear and nothing would show up on that first repeat CAT scan. When the results showed only a minor decrease in tumor size, we were obviously disappointed. Soon after the scan results, I found this verse in the book of James. "When you ask, you do not receive, because you ask with wrong motives, that you may spend what you get on your pleasures" (4:3).

I realized my prayers were definitely selfish. I did not want to go through this pain with my son. I wanted God to remove this trial from our lives. Who would want to go through over three years of fighting cancer with her son, right? Then it dawned on me that if God had answered my original prayer to remove all the tumors and traces of the cancer in Connor that first month, I would not have been much help to another family in our church whose son was diagnosed with cancer later that month. A light bulb went off in my head: I now understood the full meaning of 2 Corinthians 1:3-4.

Many times I have wondered why Connor's battle against cancer was so long, painful, and unclear. Why couldn't Connor have gotten to NED (no evidence of disease) like many of the other neuroblastoma patients? Why didn't his tumors shrink enough for the surgeons to remove them all? The "gray" area of being "not too sick but not completely healed" was daunting and frustrating. Perhaps now I have an answer to those questions. Maybe it was just for this reason in 2 Corinthians, so that we could give comfort to others who were going through similar battles. So, we will march on in this battle against cancer, and we will look for other fallen patients along this path to whom we can offer God's comfort, guidance, and hope.

Facing Reality

And whatever you do, whether in word or deed, do it all in the name of the Lord Jesus, giving thanks to God the Father through him.

—Colossians 3:17

Following is a journal entry that Tait wrote:

As I reflect upon what my family has been through over the last 106 weeks—all the clinic visits, nights at the hospital, chemotherapy, radiation, procedures ranging from finger pokes to bone marrow transplants, visits to Harvard and New York City and now down to Houston, and so on—I come away with one word: thankfulness, because my son is alive. I am both thankful and grateful that my son is alive today, 106 weeks later.

With everything going on in his life, I had a dark moment a week ago when I finally saw the report of the latest CT scan. Mind you, the CT scan hasn't changed much since the original diagnosis except that 70 percent of the original tumor was resected. However, there is still evidence of disease inside him in the remaining tumors. Whether or not those tumors still have live cancer cells is yet to be seen.

One of my great friends, a urologist, called me and informed me, much to his horror, of how bad this situation really was and still could be with Connor. I came away from that conversation with him thinking, *Wow, the child we see in person is different from the kid we see on paper.* And I had a grateful heart again, for this child is alive today because of God. The beautiful Psalm David wrote "I will extol the Lord at all times; His praise will always be on my lips . . ." is my message this week (Psalm 34:1-3). I am grateful that my son is alive and taking swimming lessons, doing karate, attending vacation bible school, wrapping up baseball season, having Nerf missile fights at night, and engaging in some serious wrestling matches with his brothers and me.

When you get weary from facing these battles again and again, a grateful heart is good medicine.

"NED"

> *Therefore do not be anxious, saying, "What shall we eat?"*
> *or "What shall we drink?" or "What shall we wear?" For the*
> *Gentiles seek after all these things, and your heavenly Father*
> *knows that you need them all. But seek first the kingdom*
> *of God and His righteousness, and all these things will be*
> *added to you. Therefore do not be anxious about tomorrow,*
> *for tomorrow will be anxious for itself. Today has enough*
> *worries of its own."*
>
> —Matthew 6:31-34

Following is a journal entry I wrote during those months of low dose treatment for Connor:

As I read websites, I learn about other children's battles with neuroblastoma. Many of these children I do not know personally, but I do feel as if I know them, and I know the battles they fight every day. I rejoice with each family whose child has reached a state of NED (no evidence of disease). It is such a relief to know that the treatment has been successful for them. But, even these families cannot fully enjoy this victory; they must anxiously wait for several years to see if their child is truly cancer free.

Although Connor has not achieved NED and I know his battle is far from over, I can't help but rejoice in the fact that his disease is not progressing. I don't think I realized how significant that was until recently. Over the last few months, I have read on many websites about children who have relapsed or have had disease progression, and many have lost their battle with cancer. My heart breaks after I read each blog post. And then I look at Connor, who looks and feels so *great* right now! Thank you, God, for that miracle!

How can it be? It's as if all the rules and norms of neuroblastoma don't apply to him right now. The doctors say he should feel sick or tired or have pain, yet he has none of these symptoms. With the amount of tumors he has, the cancer should be growing, yet it isn't. It is unlikely that he would still respond to chemotherapy, yet he still does. All I can say is "Thank You, God!" I know this is a gift from Him. I'm trying to repay Him for this gift by being grateful for Connor's exuberance, for his love of life and his love of God. I try not to dwell on the uncertainty of our future, as God tells us in Matthew 6. Instead, I enjoy every beautiful moment He has given us, and I keep my faith strong by trusting in the Lord.

Perspective

For we are God's workmanship, created in Christ Jesus to do
good works, which God prepared in advance for us to do.
—Ephesians 2:10

Following is a journal entry I wrote:

Connor's teacher has been tutoring him a couple of days a week after school to help him catch up with things he missed last year due to his treatment. I'm so impressed with him. He is really improving quickly. I'm so grateful that all of that chemotherapy did not damage his thinking and learning abilities. Praise God!

Also, Connor's hearing was tested at school the other day, and he passed! This was a child whose high-frequency hearing was severely destroyed by the chemo during his transplant. That just confirms what the ENT found when he tested Connor. What a miracle! He doesn't even wear his hearing aids in class now. He still has some hearing loss, but as long as he sits in the front row, he can hear his teacher. I guess "permanent hearing loss" isn't much of an obstacle to God. Connor just continues to baffle the doctors.

I received a devotional from Dr. James Denison that speaks of the very same thing:

> So much of life is perspective. Rain is good for the farmer
> and bad for the golfer. When your computer crashes you
> lose time but your computer repair guy makes money.
> For someone to win, someone has to lose.
>
> Except with God. He redeems everything He allows
> or causes. His brothers could sell him into slavery, but
> Joseph would later assure them, *"You intended to harm*
> *me, but God intended it for good to accomplish what is now*
> *being done, the saving of many lives"* (Genesis 50:20). The
> only way to prove that angels can stop lions is to follow
> God into their den. The only way to know that God can
> stop a flooded river is to walk into that river by faith.

So give your guilt or grief, struggle or sin, decision or dilemma to your Father. He's ready to redeem it for His glory and your good.[3]

Isn't that awesome and so true? God can truly use Connor's situation and turn it into something good for His glory. Only God can redeem something as horrible as neuroblastoma.

Be Still

Be still and know that I am God.

—Psalm 46:10

Following is a journal entry I wrote:

Tait and I feel as if we've entered a new season in our lives. For the last couple of years, everything centered on getting Connor well. Everything else was secondary, so certain activities did not exist for us. Our kids were not enrolled in sports at certain times, and our daughter, MacKenzie, did not get to participate in some extracurricular activities at school. We did not attend things that interfered with Connor's schedule. Actually, our life was simplified.

But now that Connor's treatment is less intense, we find ourselves faced with more time, which means our family has many new options and activities. So, we have filled up our new free time. It's amazing that when we are suddenly given this gift of more spare time, we tend to fill up that time and fill up our days. I feel as if I've joined the human masses on a super highway of rushed activities. We rush from here to there, and sometimes it feels like a frantic pace. I've spoken with many other families who feel the same way, so I know we're not alone. In his book, *Be Still*, Chuck Swindoll says the following: "Noise and words and frenzied hectic schedules dull our senses, closing our ears to his still, small voice and making us numb to His touch."[4]

My prayer for you and for myself is that we do not let our schedules get in the way of the most important thing . . . our relationship with God, our alone time with Him. I pray that I do not lose sight of this!

Thankfulness

> *Praise the LORD, my soul; all my inmost being, praise His holy name. Praise the LORD, my soul, and forget not all His benefits—who forgives all your sins and heals all your diseases, who redeems your life from the pit and crowns you with love and compassion, who satisfies your desires with good things so that your youth is renewed like the eagle's.*
> —Psalm 103:1-5

During a time of remission in 2008, Tait asked Connor if he remembered what happened three years ago, and he said that he didn't. With further prompting, he remembered being in a hospital but could not recall many of the details. He didn't remember the thirty days he spent in the hospital and the seven days of continuous chemo. He didn't remember the nose bleeds that wouldn't stop without a platelet transfusion or not being able to see his younger brothers because they were not allowed in the bone marrow unit. All he could remember was playing with Daddy in his hospital room and asking Jesus into his heart on Thanksgiving Day. Wow! What a blessing for him. We are so thankful that God has mercifully erased those bad memories and only left him with good ones. That is truly the peace that only comes from God.

Use Me

> *And they overcame him by the blood of the Lamb and by the*
> *word of their testimony.*
> —*Revelation 12:11*

During Connor's first round of chemo in 2005, a woman approached me in the grocery store and introduced herself as Vivian. She told me that her son was a student at Connor's school, and she shared a beautiful story with me.

Vivian had been praying for her son's attitude to change. During his senior year of high school, he had become very self-centered and was having trouble feeling empathy for others. She was concerned for him and began praying for an opportunity for him to "step out from his own little world." She specifically prayed that God would cultivate a servant's heart within her son.

The following day she came home from work to find her son sitting quietly alone in their den. As she approached him, she realized his hair was gone—it had been completely shaved off! He quickly explained, "Mom, there's this four-year-old boy at my school who has cancer. He lost his hair because of his chemo treatments, and now he's bald. Several of us on the football team decided we'd make him feel better by shaving off our hair."

Vivian told me that her son had always obsessed over his hair, carefully styling it each morning and using more hair products than she did. She explained that the shaving of his hair was the first selfless act she'd ever seen from her son. She thought it was truly a miracle that God would use a little boy to answer her prayer and change her son's heart.

You never know how God will use your trials to reach others. Some of my friends have said they like reading the Scriptures I post on my website, or sometimes they tell me that things I write help them through something difficult they are going through. I'm so grateful for those comments, because I feel like that is what God is calling me to do—encourage others and be a faithful witness to His awesome work in our lives.

I love this quote from Francis J. Roberts: "I prepare you in order to USE you in the hour of crisis. The crisis is not the time to cry for deliverance, saying, 'Lord save me,' but to cry, 'Lord, USE me.'"[5]That is what I pray for . . . "Lord, USE me."

Chapter 6

A Different Type of Surrender

I read an article recently that explained the deep meaning behind the word *surrender*. It is derived from the Greek word *paradidomi*, and Strong's Concordance offers these definitions: 1. to yield upward, 2. to transmit, and 3. to entrust.

In the world's eyes, surrender is equal to defeat. But in God's eyes, surrender precedes victory. Surrender signifies the end of pride and the end of striving. In my personal battle for my son's life, surrender meant accepting once and for all that Connor's life has always been in God's hands. It was a conscious decision to submit my will to God's will, knowing that He can see beyond my situation, and I cannot. If you think about it, isn't this the same process we all go through with our children as we guide and teach them? As parents, we ask them to trust us when we, in our experience, already know what their choices will bring. Surrender is not equal to admitting defeat; instead it is the equivalent of handing the wheel of an out-of-control car to an expert driver.

Perhaps the most perfect example of surrender is provided for us in the garden of Gethsemane when Jesus asks for a way out of the trial ahead of Him but willingly accepts His fate. At times, as I faced gut-wrenching decisions about Connor's future, I felt as if I would collapse any moment from the emotional pain. In these times, I thought of Jesus and the pain He experienced on the cross—a pain so great that no human could ever experience or understand it. Knowing this, I realized that I had to trust my Savior with the life of my son.

Connor spent about six months on the treatment plan that the doctors in New York set out for him. That was followed by almost two blissfully normal years. Connor was being treated in Houston, and his therapy was a low-dose, low-intensity treatment that kept his disease stable (and hopefully dead). This afforded him some time of normalcy as a young boy. The doctors in Houston were cautiously optimistic. We were seeing signs of a bright future on the horizon.

On December 23, 2008, our horizon changed once again. Connor's blood count was low, and the doctors felt like he was developing a stomach ulcer. The scan revealed a tumor poking into his stomach, causing a bleeding ulcer. At first glance, this did not appear to be neuroblastoma but a different type of cancer or a benign tumor. Three weeks later, we had a new diagnosis . . . malignant peripheral nerve sheath tumor. This new cancer was caused by the radiation that treated the original neuroblastoma tumor. My son, at the age of eight, was diagnosed with a second cancer. What were the odds? This news was unspeakable, unbelievable.

In January, surgeons tried to remove the new tumor. The only cure for this type of cancer is complete removal. As the surgeon greeted us in the waiting room after surgery, he felt sure that he had removed all the new cancer. But, once again, our celebration would be brief. The pathology results showed that this new cancer had grown into his old, inoperable neuroblastoma tumor. All I could think at the time was, *you have got to be kidding me!*

This began our mad dash to find a cure or any type of treatment that would stop this new tumor from growing. My son had a new dragon to slay, and this one was even more frightening than the first. We contacted doctors all over the country. None could offer any hope. This new cancer was so aggressive and fast growing. We could literally see it expanding in Connor's abdomen. One of the doctors said that a cancer created by radiation was like a monster on steroids. I believed him.

We eventually traveled to Guatemala for an immunotherapy treatment. It was our final effort, a desperate act to save our son. It was at this critical point that I came face-to-face with my own insufficiency and began to understand and experience the complete sufficiency of Christ. It was time to surrender my will to His.

Setbacks and Shadows

> *For every child of God defeats this evil world by trusting Christ to give the victory.*
>
> —John 5:4

Following is a journal entry I wrote:

We received news that Connor's tumor is still progressing. This is not the answer from God that we wanted, but I know God is still good! I prayed that God would reveal Himself to me—that He would give me answers to my many questions. I told my mom that it seems like He is just not answering our prayers right now. God seems inactive. After this conversation with my mom, I started my lesson for the week from my Bible study, The Amazing Collection. It was on the book of Esther. I felt like this lesson was speaking right to my situation. I will share with you some quotes from the study.

Here's the life application for the book of Esther:

When God's voice can't be heard, His hand can be seen. God is at work behind the scenes, protecting His people. He uses people to accomplish His plan, and His timing is always perfect.

At times, God seems to stand in the shadows. But given a chance, wouldn't we much rather experience Him standing in the light? We feel more confident when we can see Him clearly, assured that everything will work out for good. But if the book of Esther teaches us anything, it is that sometimes God works incognito—though just as mightily as ever—with His providence concealed. God's unseen hand at work is a Timeless Principle. [1]

I have to remind myself repeatedly that God is still there working for Connor and me, even when I can't see or hear Him. This quote from Oswald Chambers was also in the lesson and explains how I feel:

"But no matter how hard we look and listen, there are times in life when God remains hidden. Often we think it is failure on our part—that we must not have tried hard enough. But we have to understand that silence and mystery are part of the nature of God. And it is in those times that we must trust what we cannot see—His faithfulness—and hope for what we cannot feel—His mercy. Even in the darkness, we can rest in His love."

Wow! Even in this dark time, God is still faithful to reassure me with messages from His Word.

In His Hand

So do not fear, for I am with you; do not be dismayed, for I am your God. I will strengthen you and help you; I will uphold you with My righteous right hand.

—Isaiah 41:10

In celebration of his fortieth birthday, Tait invited my father to join him on a big-game hunting trip to Tanzania. While hunting one day, they became separated and wound up about 125 yards apart, with a herd of buffalo right in front of them in tall grass. The buffalo smelled my dad and began to charge straight toward Tait and the two trackers with him.

Tait recalls what happened next:

As we stood in front of three small trees waiting for the other hunting party, the herd broke, and the earth began to tremble. The tall grass in front of me parted as forty-five buffalo came barreling right toward me. With the herd of animals spread out thirty feet wide and running at us at twenty miles per hour, we had nowhere to run. I tried to run to the left, but the tracker grabbed me and held me behind him and the other tracker, who was trying to hide behind the small trees. The herd, which was easily breaking down larger trees in its way, was right on us.

When the black cloud of dust surrounding the animals was five to ten yards away, the buffalo miraculously moved to the left and to my right. They flew right by me! Sometimes they were as close as three feet away. I can remember the smell of their breath, the heat coming off their black coats, and the earth shaking for almost ten seconds prior to their approach. The look in their eyes was wild and terrifying. I was reminded of the African saying: "Buffalo look at you like you owe them money." My tracker pulled me closer to make room for the big bulls' wide horns. Still, one of them brushed my sleeve as it passed. As the two-thousand-pound animals crossed the plain, they forged a road through the terrain, trampling everything in their paths. I knew when they were on me, at five yards away, that my life was over. I knew and felt it. Strangely, as fear enveloped me, I suddenly had a sense of calm. It was as if I heard God say to me, "Do not fear; I have you in My hand, just as I have Connor in my hand." Our brush with certain death was the closest call that the trackers and the professional hunter had ever heard of or seen. As the roar of the herd diminished in the distance, I was left with the unshakable confirmation that God is in control and that I need not fear.

What are you afraid of today? Do you know that your omnipotent, ever-present, almighty heavenly Father has you in the palm of His hand? Confess your greatest worries and fears to Him today. You were created for a purpose, and He will see that purpose to its completion.

The New Normal

Even though I walk through the darkest valley, I will fear
no evil, for You are with me; Your rod and Your staff, they
comfort me.—Psalm 23:4

Following is a journal entry that Tait wrote soon after Connor's second cancer diagnosis:

During visits to hospitals in Dallas, Houston, Boston, New York, and Fort Worth, with the primary neuroblastoma tumor and the growth of a completely new tumor, we found that our source of rest is only in the Lord. At the end of the day, we will fight until there is no more fight. The only way we are getting through the dark nights, thoughts that we don't want in our brain, questions we don't want to have to answer, and doctors we do not want to have to see is through your prayers, your encouragement, and knowing that our Lord is giving us strength.

Early on in this fight I quoted Psalm 23, saying we are going through the valley of darkness; to our right is dark, and to our left is dark. Our old life, our old "normal," is behind us, and the new normal ahead of us is black. The only way we're getting through this is with your fingerprints all over us, pushing us through this. Today, as the father of an eight-year-old son who has two dragons inside him trying to devour him, I say thank you. After forty-six months of fighting, hundreds of visits to the doctor, thousands of pills, gallons of chemo, and countless surgeries, Connor has never complained.

My question to you today is, what do you have to complain about? I'm asking you to be grateful, to embrace life's challenges, and to say a prayer for an eight-year-old boy who is fighting cancer, and also, I say thank you for your incredible faithfulness in lifting up our family.

Emerging from the Darkness

He who dwells in the shelter of the Most High will rest in the shadow of the Almighty. I will say of the Lord, He is my refuge and my fortress, my God, in whom I trust.
—*Psalm 91:1-2*

Following is a journal entry I wrote after the reality of the second diagnosis started to set in.

At first glance, this trial seems like a curse or a dark valley where no light can shine. As we continue on this difficult, dark journey, we see so much light . . . light in the forms of guidance, love, support, answered prayers, peace, beauty, and joy in the midst of suffering. It's as if life is more vibrant now. Many things hold more significant meaning to me. God's peace, joy, faithfulness, and love toward my family and me; thankfulness for my many blessings and each new day; contentment in all situations; and total reliance on God are just a few things that resonate fully for me now. I've always known these truths, but now I experience and live them daily. "I once was blind, but now I see." This new part of our journey is definitely daunting and scary, but our faith remains strong even after this second "D-day" (d for diagnosis). This quote from Francis De Sales from The Amazing Collection sums up how we are trusting in God to carry us:

"Do not look forward to the changes and chances of this life in fear; rather look to them with full hope that, as they arise, God, whose you are, will deliver you out of them. He is your keeper. He has kept you hitherto. Do you but hold fast to His dear hand, and He will lead you safely through all things; and when you cannot stand, He will bear you in His arms."

If I Live to Tell

Yet he did not waver through unbelief regarding the promise of God, but was strengthened in his faith and gave glory to God, being fully persuaded that God had power to do what he had promised.

—Romans 4:20

I do believe; help me overcome my unbelief.

—Mark 9:24

Following is a journal entry I wrote before we set off for Guatemala:

We are swinging for the fence. It's the ninth inning, and we are putting in the pinch hitter, so to speak. There have been many miracles in Guatemala, and the doctor here is a godly man who gives all credit for healing miracles to God. I like a man who gives credit where credit is due. We prayerfully considered this treatment in Guatemala and we feel peace that this is where God is leading us. We believe that if we are in God's will and following His path for our lives, we know He will surround us with His love and will not leave us.

We know that Connor's destiny will soon be revealed. No more waiting to see God's hand. No more God working behind the scenes. His plans for Connor will come to fruition soon. His healing is on the way; whether it is healing on earth or in heaven, my son will not be suffering much longer. I still believe that he will be healed here on earth. I believe God has a special plan and purpose to be worked out through his life here on earth. What a story he will live to tell.

I recently heard a song called "I Have to Believe" by Rita Springer. The song describes God's unbelievable omniscient, omnipresent qualities. In our deepest pain, He knows our needs before we speak them. In our darkest nights, we are never left alone. What greater comfort can we have than God's presence in our lives?

The Point of Surrender

*Call upon Me in the day of trouble; I will deliver you, and
you will honor Me.*

—Psalm 50:15

The story of King Jehoshaphat in 2 Chronicles 20 is a great example
of corporate prayer. When the King found out a huge enemy was
coming against him, he asked all the people to fast and pray in order
to defeat the enemy. The King said in verse 12, "For we have no
power to face this vast army that is attacking us. We do not know
what to do, but our eyes are on you."

I can relate to King Jehoshaphat's words. This cancer is like a great
enemy, and we don't know what to do. Yet, when I read beyond the
King's declaration, I am faced with God's truth. The prophet Jahaziel
spoke these words from the Lord: "You will not have to fight this
battle. Take up your positions; stand firm and see the deliverance
the LORD will give you, Judah and Jerusalem. Do not be afraid; do
not be discouraged. Go out to face them tomorrow, and the LORD
will be with you.'" (verse 17). He told them to stand still and sing
His praises. That was His strategy for fighting the enemy! The King
appointed those who should sing to the Lord and those who should
praise His beauty and holiness. They went out before the army
saying, "Give thanks to the Lord for his love endures forever" (verse
21). The Lord delivered them from their enemy.

Following is a journal entry I wrote around the time I read these
verses:

> This week, please pray for Connor and sing God's praises.
> Thank Him for His mercy, grace, provision, strength, and
> peace that He has provided us with during this trial. As
> King Hezekiah and the people of Israel witnessed, may
> God also deliver Connor from his enemy, cancer.

Staying in the Sweet Spot

Again, I tell you that if two of you on earth agree about anything you ask for, it will be done for you by My Father in heaven. For where two or three come together in My name, there am I with them.

—Matthew 18:19-20

Following is a journal entry I wrote when we arrived in Guatemala:

Thank you to everyone who stopped by the house Sunday. A good friend of ours led us in songs of worship and praise on his guitar and in a prayer time for Connor. It was beautiful seeing our family room full of family and friends singing and praying for Connor. I can only imagine that God was pleased with our praise. It was a perfect example of praising Him during a storm.

I now know what the Bible means when it says that God gives us "a peace that passes all understanding." Not only do we feel a peace that is inconceivable in terms of what the world can understand, but we feel a peace in spite of *our* lack of understanding. We have peace even though we don't understand why any of this is happening. Peace that only God can give.

We feel totally at peace with this new direction for Connor's treatment. Feelings of expectancy and joy are filling me as I look forward to what God is going to do. I can't explain it. When we gave our testimony last week, I mentioned that there is this "sweet spot" that I yearn for . . . where no fear or doubt can penetrate. In this place, you are so focused on eternal things that what you see with your eyes doesn't compare to your knowledge of God's presence. Just knowing that He will never let go fills me with hope and peace. I pray that God will keep Connor and my family in this sweet spot as we continue on our journey.

Thanks for the prayers, love, and support from everyone. Keep the prayers coming.

Now Is the Time

> *Even youths grow tired and weary and young men stumble and fall; but those who hope in the Lord will renew their strength. They will soar on wings like eagles; they will run and not grow weary, they will walk and not be faint.*
> —Isaiah 40:30-31

Following is another of my journal entries:

> I was listening to the song "The Time of My Life" by David Cook a couple of days ago. After really listening to the words, it struck me how we are all waiting on something until we can proceed or succeed. When Connor was first diagnosed, we postponed so many things, saying, "We'll do that when Connor is better." I think we often miss out on blessings when we are waiting to act. We often think we will find happiness when the trial has passed or we'll be strong when we are not so weary or tired. But God promises us something different in His Word.
>
> Now, with Connor fighting this new cancer, it's even more likely that we will delay God's plan or miss His blessings for us. Tait and I could say that we will believe Connor is healed when we can see all the evidence that confirms that belief. Or we can cling to the promise in Hebrews 11:1. "Now faith is being sure of what we hope for and certain of what we do not see."
>
> So often in life, we make little mental proclamations to ourselves, such as, "I will forgive her when she apologizes"; "I will be happy when I lose fifteen pounds"; or "I will start enjoying all the blessings God has given me after He answers this one prayer request." We need to put an end to this way of thinking! Through God, we have the ability to do all these things right now. We can forgive *now*. We can believe *now*. We can have joy *now*. We can be strong *now*. We can praise Him *now*.

I sound like I'm on a soap box, but we are all missing out on God's ability to work through us and His willingness to bless us. We just have to plug in to Him, and our time is now. This could be the time of our lives. So, stop waiting!

Created for a Purpose

> *The LORD will fulfill [his purpose] for me; Your love, O LORD, endures forever—do not abandon the works of Your hands.*
>
> —Psalm 138:8

When the *whys* come, we have to realize that life still has purpose, that we were created for a purpose. Knowing that God had a special purpose for Connor (designed especially for him before he was even born) helped me feel secure in times of anxiety and trouble.

Here is another of my journal entries:

> I guess we have reached a point where we are "leaving it all out on the field" in our fight for Connor. No stone unturned. We will diligently seek God's direction in Connor's treatment, diligently seek His face, do everything possible to help Connor in this fight . . . and then lay it all at Jesus' feet. God knew the number of Connor's days before he was even born, whether those days would add up to eight years or eighty.
>
> We will rest in the knowledge that God loves Connor more than we do and that He has a special plan for him. We still believe that God is going to save Connor. We will remain steadfast. We are praying God will use these new drugs as he used the Israelites when they were marching around Jericho. Like the walls of Jericho, this cancer will crumble.

Decisions

Trust in the LORD with all your heart, and do not lean on
your own understanding, in all your ways acknowledge Him,
and He will make straight your paths.

—Proverbs 3:5-6

Over the past four years, I have learned that God takes us down many unforeseen roads, unexplained directions, and confusing paths. In our limited view, it is all perplexing, but God never does anything the way our simple minds imagine.

Consider the story of Joshua. Can you imagine what the Israelites thought when God told them to just walk around the city of Jericho, and the walls would fall? I'm sure it sounded crazy to them, but God wanted to take them on a path that would give Him the most glory. It was a strange, unforgettable, and questionable plan, but He worked it out! Connor's four-year journey through cancer certainly did not follow the "typical" path that the doctors predicted. (At the time of Connor's initial diagnosis, he was only given three months to live.) Instead, Connor's path was swerving, confusing, unique, and filled with mini-miracles along the way. But, maybe that was the best path of all—one that only had answers in God's strength, His healing power, and His sovereignty. Did you happen to notice what the verse from Proverbs instructs us to do in order to receive God's guidance? We must acknowledge Him in all our ways. I believe this is God's way of asking for our undivided attention. If we want Him to direct us, we must trust Him completely and give Him honor and glory in every aspect of our lives: our relationships, our finances, our thoughts, and our desires. When we do this, we can be assured that, as long as we are on God's path, we are going the right way.

Someone Else's Miracle

I have set the Lord always before me; because He is at my right hand, I will not be shaken.

—Psalm 16:8

Following is a journal entry I wrote after we met the doctor in Guatemala for the first time:

The first day we arrived in Guatemala, we met several of the patients. When we went in to meet the doctor, all the patients in the waiting room stood in a circle and prayed for Connor. The doctor was praying for Connor. What a place of faith! It is exactly where we need to be.

How refreshing this was compared to the words of imminent disaster that I normally hear from doctors! The doctor is not making big promises. He just says to pray that God will make this work. I told him that we are praying and that thousands of others are, too.

The second day, a woman got the great news that she was now free of breast cancer. As she made her announcement, the patients gathered around her and bowed their heads—giving thanks to the One who deserves the credit for healing her.

We felt that God was letting us witness a miracle. I cried along with the rest of the room, though I didn't even know her.

Beyond the Valley

*"Though the mountains be shaken and the hills be removed,
yet My unfailing love for you will not be shaken nor My
covenant of peace by removed," says the LORD, who has
compassion on you.*

—Isaiah 54:10

Oh, how fear can take hold of us in dark moments! Watching my
sweet Connor slipping away from us more and more each day
brought fresh fear with each glance. I could not hide the fact that I
was afraid of what would come to pass.

Each of us will face the last struggling days of a loved one at
one time or another, whether it be a grandparent, sibling, parent,
or friend. It is inevitable that we each will face these fears. I cried
out to God every time fear overcame me. I think I was in constant
communion with God for the last two months of Connor's life. It
was the only way to keep fear from completely overwhelming me.

Rescue

*They loathed all food and drew near the gates of death. Then
they cried to the LORD in their trouble, and He saved them
from their distress. He sent forth His word and healed them;
He rescued them from the grave. Let them give thanks to the
LORD for His unfailing love and His wonderful deeds for
mankind. Let them sacrifice thank offerings and tell of His
works with songs of joy.*

—Psalm 107:17-22

In the last month before Connor's passing, he wasn't eating very
much. He didn't feel hungry, and he said that food did not taste
good to him. When I read the Psalm above, it spoke to me. "They
loathed all food"—it's as if Connor was speaking those very words
to himself.

In the midst of the worst of circumstances, I took this verse to
heart. It was my mantra. I cried out to the Lord, because only He
could help us. I knew that healing would come one way or another.
Because of Christ's love for us, He has conquered the grave. Facing
the possible death of my son, I clung to the knowledge that Connor
was taken care of, either by healing on earth or in heaven. Relying
on this assurance cast out my fears and allowed me to face the
oncoming days with peace. What joy God's perfect peace brings!
Knowing that our Father in heaven can provide peace and hope in
the midst of our worst nightmares is a comfort like no other.

Chapter 7

The Battle versus the War

Bishop J. C. Ryle once said, "If tomorrow brings a cross, God will send you the grace to bear it." Connor struggled with his second cancer for almost seven months. Our desperate search for a cure was met time after time with elusive, disappointing treatments. Nothing worked. Nothing slowed the disease's progression.

On July 10, 2009, while surrounded by his family, closest friends, and a waiting room filled with his faithful prayer warriors, our Connor went to be with the Lord. My son journeyed well. He honored God. He never complained. He lived his short life to the fullest, and he died with the security of knowing that the moment his eyes closed on earth, they would open in the presence of His Lord and Savior.

God's molding, refining, and sculpting continues in our lives. We are constantly seeking His face and His enlightenment during these trying times. We continue to learn more about God, His ways, and His character, while sitting humbled and broken at His feet.

We have learned that we are not forsaken because healing didn't come. For God has clearly told us, "Never will I leave you; never will I forsake you" (Hebrews 13:5). And I am seeing firsthand that this is true. While our hope was initially in Connor's healing on earth, our hope changed as we aligned our will with God's will.

I truly believe that God wants to give us the desires of our hearts (Psalm 34:7). It's easy to ask for them. It can be difficult to accept God's answer when it looks very different from the one for which we've spent four years praying.

There is great comfort in knowing that while we may have lost this battle, the *war* has been won. On the cross of Calvary, Jesus Christ conquered sin and death once and for all. Because of His great sacrifice, I will see my Connor again—healed, complete, and glorified in the presence of the Lord for eternity.

Surrendering My Will

The righteous person may have many troubles, but the LORD
delivers him from them all;
—Psalm 34:19

The week leading up to Connor's journey home to the Lord was very stressful. His feeding tube had fallen out on July 4, and he was not getting any nutrients; he was severely dehydrated due to the fluids and food that were flushing right through him. That whole week, we spent every day at the hospital, trying to fix the feeding tube—but to no avail. Five days later, a procedure was done at the hospital where another feeding tube was placed in Connor's abdomen. When we arrived home, we realized the new tube was leaking and the procedure did not fix the problem.

Shortly after we realized this, I got a phone call from the doctor in regard to Connor's lab work. His red blood count and platelets were low again, so he would have to go back to the hospital for more blood and platelets. The doctor also informed me that his BUN level was extremely high, which meant Connor was dangerously dehydrated. If he started hallucinating or became non-responsive, we were to bring him into the ER as soon as possible. At this point, I was so worn out. It didn't matter how hard I tried to fix these problems—to fix Connor. If God didn't choose to heal Connor, it was all in vain. I could only do so much. It was like running on a treadmill. I was spending all this energy and all this time, but I wasn't making any progress for Connor. Outside on our patio, Mom, Tait, and I prayed. We prayed that God would either heal Connor or take him home. We were not selfish enough to want to keep Connor here the way he was. If His ultimate plan was not to heal Connor, then we wanted God to relieve him of his suffering. We surrendered our precious Connor into God's hands and prayed for a sign. Two hours later, Connor became non-responsive. We called the ambulance, which led us to Children's Medical Center and Connor's last twenty-four hours.

My daughter, MacKenzie, in her wisdom, read this verse to Connor on his last day. Jesus was in the garden of Gethsemane, waiting for the soldiers to come take him. He said to his Father in heaven, "My Father, if it is possible, may this cup be taken from me. Yet not as I will, but as you will" (Matthew 26:39). It is so hard to relinquish what we love so much to God. We want to hold on with all we have to what we hold dear. It was so hard to let Connor go, yet we knew in our hearts it was right.

Never Hunger and Thirst Again

> *They hunger no longer, nor thirst anymore; nor does the sun beat down on them, nor any heat; for the Lamb in the center of the throne is the Shepherd, and guides them to springs of the water of life; and God wipes every tear from their eyes.*
> —Revelation 7:16-17

During the final days of Connor's illness, he ate and drank constantly. He would even drink throughout the night, finishing off several cups of water, juice, soda, and Gatorade. He would make me drive him to 7-Eleven or the grocery store, and we would go through each aisle until he had chosen his drinks for the next twenty-four hours. He was almost obsessed with having enough drinks on hand. Months after his passing, I could still see evidence of his drink selections in my pantry.

When I think of Connor this way, I can't help but think of John 6:35. "Then Jesus declared, 'I am the bread of life. He who comes to Me will never go hungry, and he who believes in Me will never be thirsty.'" Connor's physical state was hungry and thirsty all the time, and he was never fully satisfied. He was always searching for physical fulfillment. His condition reminds me of the emptiness of the human heart without Christ. How many times do we seek after something that will fulfill us, only to be left feeling empty? Recently, I was watching an interview with a popular music artist on television. She said, "All of us are moving toward a place of happiness; isn't that what we ultimately strive for in life?" I couldn't help but think how she is chasing after the wrong dream. She will never find the happiness she seeks without a personal relationship with God. She will continue to thirst and hunger until God fills that need in her life. He is the only One who can complete us.

I am glad to know that Connor is now fully satisfied, never to thirst or hunger again. God's promise offers a comforting future for Connor and for all of us. When we tap into the only true source of fulfillment, God will meet all our needs—physical and spiritual—now and for eternity.

The Race

He will swallow up death for all time, and the Lord GOD will
wipe tears away from all faces.
—Isaiah 25:8

Shortly after Connor went to be with the Lord, my husband Tait and I traveled to Connecticut to participate in a relay race benefiting the charity we founded in our son's honor. In the annual TeamConnor 500, runners take turns running five-mile legs until they reach the goal of five hundred miles. It is a tradition for Tait and I to end the race. As we completed the last five miles of the relay, we ran uphill for approximately one-eighth of a mile, unable to see the finish line. And then we began hearing the noise. At first, it was a distant whisper. Then it slowly grew louder. And finally we began to distinguish it: the shouts of encouragement and joy. The clapping and cheering conveyed everyone's love and support. Eventually, familiar faces came into view. Smiles beamed as they cheered us on toward the finish line. It was an instant adrenaline rush of love, joy, and accomplishment.

As we crossed the finish line, I thought, *this must be what it is like to enter heaven (times one-thousand or a million)!* How wonderful Connor must have felt to have family and friends cheering him toward his eternal home! He must have been beaming! I can imagine his little legs picking up pace, running faster than he ever had. I'm sure that as Connor approached, people were slapping him high-five's and giving him "knuckles." They were patting him on the back and cheering. But that wouldn't be the best part. Imagine the group of well-wishers separating, forming two lines to usher Connor down the center toward his biggest fan. At the end of the line, he would come face-to-face with his Savior. Can you comprehend looking up into those eyes? Wow! I don't even know how to describe what that must have felt like. Knowing Connor, he probably reached out and gave Jesus one of his famous, fantastic hugs. Oh, what a hug that must have been! I'm sure Connor felt loved and cherished as never before. As much as we miss Connor, Tait and I would never wish him back here—back to the challenges and pain that this life offered him. Never would we wish him away from the One who loves him more than anyone else. True comfort and peace can only be found in the assurance of heaven for those who believe.

Worse Than Death

> *No, in all these things we are more than conquerors through*
> *Him who loved us. 38 For I am convinced that neither death*
> *nor life, neither angels nor demons, neither the present nor*
> *the future, nor any powers,*
>
> —Romans 8:37-38

Before Connor passed, and even after, I felt there could be nothing worse than losing a child. I've had many people tell me they feel the same way. I have to admit that I can't imagine worse grief than this. It is heart wrenching; I could not get through this time of grief without God's grace. That being said, I have changed my mind. I believe there is something worse—spending a life and an eternity without knowing God. I can't imagine facing the trials of this world without the peace, strength, and comfort only He can provide. What would life be like without His promise for a hope and future? (Jeremiah 29:11)

Like anyone who suffers loss, I would love to reverse my situation and bring my Connor back. In fact, Carson and Mason were just talking about that in the car last week. Mason (who is four) said that we should just buy Connor back. How I wish it were that simple. We even talked about what we would do if we had Connor back for a day. It was fun to daydream. But, we are deceived by our longings for what we once had. Even if we had Connor back with us on earth, we cannot have him here with us forever. He would eventually face death. No one can avoid that one fact—death is inevitable.

I realize that the greatest enemy we face is death itself, which claims everyone and everything. No miracle can ultimately save us from it. A miracle is therefore only a temporary solution. We really need more than a miracle—we need a resurrection to make life eternally new. We long for a life in which death is finally and ultimately defeated.

Thank you, God, that death does not have the final word; life does. Jesus' death and resurrection made it possible. He now has the authority to give life to those who want and need it. In the New

Testament, there are countless stories of Jesus performing miracles and healing many people. But, eventually, all those people still faced death. In other words, Jesus' miracles were not the ultimate reason for His coming. His great victory was not His miracles, but His resurrection. Jesus guarantees that the last chapter of the human story is not death, but life. All tears and pain and sorrow will be swallowed up in everlasting life and pure, inextinguishable joy.

I'm thankful for that beautiful gift. Even though I feel the pain of my present circumstances, which remind me of what I have lost, I can still hope for future victory spent with Jesus (and Connor).

A Bigger and Better Plan

> *I eagerly expect and hope that I will in no way be ashamed,*
> *but will have sufficient courage so that now as always Christ*
> *will be exalted in my body, whether by life or by death. For*
> *to me,* to live is Christ and to die is gain.
>
> —Philippians 1:20-21

I recently completed a Bible study called "Anointed, Transformed, Redeemed." One of the authors, Beth Moore, spoke on the topic of getting past our devastation with God. It spoke to me so completely. Here is what she said:

> "Nothing has the capacity to cause more destruction in a
> believer's life than an occurrence that makes us question
> everything we thought we knew about God. A heart can
> shatter in so many pieces that we don't think even God
> could put it back together again. Words fail, but far more
> consequentially, faith often fails."[1]

We may find ourselves in a predicament in which we question God's goodness and His sovereignty. I know that Tait and I had many questions after Connor's death. I know that Satan would love nothing more than to convince us that God is not good after all.

The story of John the Baptist in prison is a good illustratration of God's sovereignty and His ultimate healing and plan for our lives—a plan for us to spend eternity with Him.

In Luke 7:18-23, John is in prison waiting to be executed, and he sends his disciples out to ask Jesus if He is truly the one they have been waiting for. Is He the Messiah? Jesus replies, "Go back and report to John what you have seen and heard: The blind receive sight, the lame walk, those who have leprosy are cleansed, the deaf hear, the dead are raised, and the good news is proclaimed to the poor. Blessed is anyone who does not stumble on account of me." (22-23) As we know from John's story, not only did Jesus allow John to be imprisoned, but He also allowed him to be executed. But, this did not cause John to "fall away" from God. Just like John, God didn't heal or rescue Connor the way we had hoped and prayed for, but God healed and rescued him in a much more miraculous way. He rescued him from sin and death for all eternity.

Just like the miracles Jesus was performing on the masses described in Luke 7, He also caused Connor's "blind" eyes to open on July 10, 2009. His eyes opened to the very face of God. He caused Connor's "lame legs" to dance on the streets of gold. No more wheelchair for Connor; He caused his "leprous" sin to be cured for all eternity.

The "dead" was indeed raised, and Connor heard the best news of all (without his hearing aids): "Welcome home, my good and faithful servant! Enter your Master's happiness!"

Sometimes there's just a bigger plan. The knowledge that God has a bigger and better plan for us gives me comfort and reminds me that God is still good—all the time.

Yearning for Home

But in keeping with His promise we are looking forward to a
new heaven and a new earth, where righteousness dwells.
—2 Peter 3:13

Suffering has created within me a special yearning for my heavenly home. I think we all have a sense of heaven, but suffering brings it to the forefront of our hearts and minds. As believers in Jesus Christ, we know that earth is not our true home—we're merely passing through.

Even at his young age, Connor had a special yearning for his real home. In the spring of 2008, Connor informed me that he wanted to go home (as we were sitting in our family room). I said to him, "We are home, silly." He replied, "No, my *real* home. God is my heavenly Father, so heaven is my real home." I said, "You're right, but are you really ready to go home now?" He smiled and answered, "Not yet, Mommy. I'm not ready yet." At the time, I wondered if our conversation was some kind of foreshadowing. I prayed that it wasn't God's preparation to get me ready for Connor's home-going. Looking back, I believe God was preparing Connor's heart for his eternal home.

I believe Connor always knew he was just passing through this place on his way home. He never slept in his own room. He slept with MacKenzie when he was really young and then Carson when he got older. He always gave all his money to Carson to put in his piggy bank, so they could share their money. He never collected baseball cards or special items. He would always give them away. Connor and Carson shared their clothes and closet. I think the closer he got to his home-going, the more he yearned for it and had a true sense of it. I can imagine that when Connor first opened his eyes to see God's face, He finally felt he was home.

A Time and Purpose

. . . being confident of this, that He who began a good work in you will carry it on to completion until the day of Christ Jesus.

—Philippians 1:6

I know that for all of us, God has a purpose. For some of us, we will have to live a long life to fulfill that purpose. For others, like Connor, our purpose doesn't require a long life.

In Sunday school recently, our teacher talked about Jesus' purpose on earth. His ministry started when He was thirty, and he had about three years until His death on the cross to complete His purpose on earth. He had to pack a whole life of ministry into three years! I never really thought about how much He accomplished in such a short time.

Our teacher also mentioned how John the Baptist prepared the way for the Messiah in his messages to the crowds. When Jesus arrived, John introduced Him and baptized Him. God spoke to the crowd at this time, announcing that Jesus was His Son. Shortly after, John was imprisoned and executed. He had fulfilled his purpose of leading the way for Jesus.

When I think of Connor, I know that God fashioned him in my womb nine years ago with a plan for his life. Because God had this plan for Connor, he was able to live out his purpose on earth in an outstanding way. I can just imagine God's saying to him, "You got your job done, so you get to come home." I ask myself today, "How well am I carrying out God's purpose in my life?" Will I have just a few short years to carry out my purpose, or will I have a long life to pursue this? Either way, I want to do my job well, just as Connor did.

Chapter 8

Battle Lessons Learned

I once read that when you experience loss, your heart expands to handle the grief. Your heart is then larger so that it can grow more, love more, and experience more. I guess it enters a raw state in which it's alive and open to every sensory experience. It's similar to what happens to our muscles when we lift weights. The muscle tears a little at first, and then it enlarges.

Tait and I can relate to this. I definitely feel my heart has expanded to handle this grief. It is feeling everything more deeply. I feel sadness more and joy more. I experience both excitement and depression to a higher degree. My heart is open and ready for growth now. It craves understanding, wisdom, and assurance. I guess because of this, I feel as though I've grown a lot in the last few months. My heart has learned many things. I've learned that although God's grace is what spares us from disaster or loss, His grace is poured out on us even more when we are not spared. I've seen several children spared from Connor's fate, and yes, God's grace spared them. However, I can tell you that if He has allowed you to experience the loss, He will provide you with the grace to survive it. I love this quote below from Dr. Alan Redpath.

> There is nothing—absolutely no circumstance, no trouble, no testing that can ever touch me until, first of

all, it has gone past God and past Christ right through to me. If it has come that far, it has come with a great purpose which I may not understand at the moment. But as I refuse to become panicky, as I lift up my eyes to Him, and I accept it as coming from the throne of God for some great purpose of blessing to my own heart, no sorrow will ever disturb me, no trial will ever disarm me, no circumstance will cause me to fret, and I shall rest in the joy of what my Lord is. That is the rest of victory.[1]

As His hand is on my life, I'm counting on God to bring me through even this to victory. I believe His grace will revive me again. "Though you have made me see troubles, many and bitter, you will restore my life again; from the depths of the earth you will again bring me up. You will increase my honor and comfort me once more" (Psalm 71:20-21).

Facing a New Beginning

"What no eye has seen, what no ear has heard, and what no human mind has conceived"—the things God has prepared for those who love Him.
—1 Corinthians 2:9

As 2009 drew to a close, I was eager for 2010 to begin. After Christmas, our family again experienced loss when a dear aunt and cousin both passed away. We had seven deaths in our family in 2009. The loss we've experienced this year is more than daunting. At times, the burden felt too large to overcome. I wanted to sprint to the finish line of 2009 and begin 2010 with a fresh start, with a renewed hope that God would restore joy and blessings to our family. I couldn't make the days fly by fast enough.

However, after speaking with a friend who also lost her four-year-old son to cancer that year, I began to see the end of 2009 in a different light. When December passes, it will be the end of the last year we shared with our son Connor. It will be the end of an era—the end of a year filled with last experiences with my son. Suddenly my perspective changed. I wanted to cling to 2009 harder than ever. I was not ready to close this chapter of my life. I began to envision the days and months of the new year pulling me farther and farther away from Connor.

As New Year's Day approached, my emotions peaked and spiraled. I desperately sought wisdom from the Lord to calm my restless spirit. Then a pastor at our church spoke on the topic of Psalm 103, which gave me a blueprint for ushering in the new year: "Praise the LORD, O my soul; all my inmost being, praise His holy name. Praise the LORD, O my soul, and forget not all His benefits—who forgives all your sins and heals all your diseases, who redeems your life from the pit and crowns you with love and compassion, who satisfies your desires with good things so that your youth is renewed like the eagle's" (verses 1-5).

Verse 1 was a personal pep talk just for me. I need those from time to time. I imagine that King David didn't feel like praising the

Lord at the time when he wrote this psalm, so he had to remind himself to do it. I can relate to that."Forget not his benefits . . ." Before I could look forward to the new year, I needed to reflect on my past and remember God's blessings and faithfulness. It's so easy to focus on all that I have lost this year, but when I look back, I can see the many blessings that God has afforded me.

"He forgives us our sins . . ." In doing so, God gives us an opportunity to spend eternity with Him. This forgiveness makes it possible for me to see Connor again. God is more concerned with where we spend our eternity than the number of days we spend on earth. What a blessing that He has provided a way for our eternal salvation.

I'm counting on the promises of verses 4 and 5. I'm ready for Him to satisfy my desires with good things. I am praying that this new year will be one of redemption and good things!

Powerless

> *Now to Him who is able to do immeasurably more than all*
> *we ask or imagine, according to His power that is at work*
> *within us.*
> —Ephesians 3:20-21

I've started to play tennis. It's a wonderful, fun sport, but it can be frustrating for a new player. A few months ago, I had a particularly maddening experience. I had just come from a Bible study class on prayer. I have to admit that my prayer life is going through some reconstruction right now. In Bible study, I confessed my doubt that prayers actually "move mountains." Feelings of frustration were bubbling within me when I stepped onto the court. The study had brought my heart's deep wounds to the surface, and I was ready to vent my feelings.

My team was in the middle of a practice drill: play until you miss a shot and then go to the end of the line. After several attempts, I found myself at the back of the line, each time vowing to make corrections and try harder. I dreaded the instructor's command, "Next!" I was beginning to feel like I was in a *Seinfeld* episode with the Soup Nazi! I wanted to stay at the front and keep trying. But, I was not allowed. *"Next!"* I was ten seconds away from stomping my feet and throwing a four-year-old fit.

I took a deep breath to get my composure. Why couldn't I control my emotions? After the practice session, I got in my car, and the tears flowed. I realized why this had been so hard for me. The feelings of frustration I felt during the last six months of Connor's life were coming to the surface and flowing over like hot lava, like my son Carson likes to say. The feeling of being powerless was overwhelming.

I bowed my head and sent up a prayer full of whys to God. Why didn't our prayers work? Why didn't our hard work pay off for Connor? I've always believed if you work hard enough for something, you can achieve it. Yet, I'm still here, willing to fight for Connor. I wasn't ready to give up . . . so why was the choice taken from me? Despite all my human effort, I was powerless to change the direction of Connor's life.

During the course of our lives, we are bound to have powerless moments . . . so how do we deal with them? I certainly don't have all the answers to these questions. I'm still struggling with all of this myself, but I have come to some conclusions.

When I come to a point of powerlessness, I must turn to God. He is completely sufficient. Maybe I was brought to this point with no helpful resources within or around me so that I would be forced back to His throne—back to the only source of power.

As Frances J. Roberts has written,

> "Many dangers beset your path, but I shall keep you if you trust in Me. Many sorrows compass you about, but I give you joy that is greater. Look not to your own abilities, for My Spirit empowers the one who would walk in faith, so that he who is weak need not despair, and he who feels himself to be strong shall learn not to boast; for I bring down the mighty and make strong the weak."[2]

The Honest Cries of Our Hearts

Have mercy on me, LORD, for I am faint; heal me, LORD,
for my bones are in agony. My soul is in deep anguish. How
long, LORD, how long? Turn, LORD, and deliver me; save
me because of Your unfailing love.

—Psalm 6:2-4

Saturday, May 15, 2010, was the five-year anniversary of Connor's original diagnosis of stage four neuroblastoma. It was the beginning of our metamorphosis, the changing of our lives forever. While I don't feel like a beautiful butterfly, I have definitely gone through a transformation.

The roaring train that began five years ago left its mark on Tait, my children, and me. I suppose that I thought when Connor's struggles ended on earth, the pain would somehow ease on my family. Instead, our youngest son, Mason, has developed anger issues. Carson deals with boredom since losing his playmate and best friend. MacKenzie has become fiercely independent and mature beyond her years, namely because Tait and I were not there for her emotionally and physically. How we wish we could ease our children's pain!While their suffering is not physical as Connor's was, it is still suffering. As a result, I've had many honest, anguished conversations with God in which I've cried, "Enough, already! Isn't our punch card full yet?"

When we received Connor's initial diagnosis, I could not envision life without him. As his treatment progressed, my visions of the future included parading him through the hospital before all the doctors who doubted he could be healed. He would be a sign to them that God is powerful, awesome, and miraculous. I was sure God's plan would best be served if Connor were healed on earth. It wasn't supposed to end this way.

In times when I allow myself to dwell on my loss, it is easy to fall into a cycle of doubting God's sovereignty and His willingness to heal in this day and time. I sometimes feel guilty for thinking this way. *Do I have the right to question God? Is it disrespectful?* Then, I think of my daughter, MacKenzie. If she had a problem—especially a problem with me—I would want her to come to me immediately so that I could help her. I have learned that God wants the same level of trust and communication from me.

The book of Job contains an incredible example of crying out to God—throwing our doubts, complaints, and worries His way. Job lamented, "Though I cry, 'I've been wronged!' I get no response; though I call for help, there is no justice. He has blocked my way so I cannot pass; He has shrouded my paths in darkness. He has stripped me of my honor and removed the crown from my head. He tears me down on every side till I am gone; He uproots my hope like a tree" (Job 19:7-10).

These honest complaints give me confidence to share my innermost worries without fear or restraint. God wants to hear our thoughts, good and bad. He wants all our hearts—not just the good and pretty pieces but also the hurting, ugly, and angry pieces. Do you need to cry out to Him today?

Journey Well

Run in such a way as to get the prize. Everyone who competes in the games goes into strict training. They do it to get a crown that will not last; but we do it to get a crown that will last forever.

—1 Corinthians 9:24-25

I have discovered something very important about prayer: our prayers should focus less on how we want our life's journey to end and more on "journeying well." A friend of mine who is battling cancer told me recently, "You can pray for healing for me if you feel led to, but my prayer for myself is that wherever God directs my journey, that I would journey well." To me, that says it all. If we are praying this way, we are seeking God's will.

When faced with a scary prognosis, an unsure future, or an overwhelming burden, our natural response is to ask God to remove the trial from our lives. We want Him to fix the situation, remove the thorn from our side. How many times did I pray that for Connor? In retrospect, I would have spent more time praying for God's grace to carry me through.

I know this is easier said than done. I was the first one down on my knees praying for Connor's healing. But let me clarify: I don't think God wants us to quit asking for the desires of our hearts, but He does want us to surrender to His will. So, as for me, when I pray for others or myself with regard to facing trials, I will pray that we would journey well. I will ask God to carry my loved ones and me through the dark valleys in life. And I will pray for His strength and grace as we walk, so that we may glorify Him as He redeems our suffering.

Frances J. Roberts had this to say about journeying well:

> "Out of much tribulation I bring forth a people for the glory of My Name. I am shaping you in the furnace of affliction that I may set My seal upon you and display in you My own identity. I desire that you be one with Me in all I have purposed, and as I move in the earth

today to redeem the lost and deliver the captives, you are moving with Me whenever your soul and spirit are yielded to Me as an open channel of prayer in the Spirit."[3]

A New Way of Praying

What is more, I consider everything a loss compared to the surpassing greatness of knowing Christ Jesus my Lord.—Philippians 3:8

I mentioned earlier that my prayer life has had an "under construction" sign around it since Connor's passing. During Connor's illness, I was always searching for Bible verses and Christian books on building a powerful prayer life. Armed with plenty of information, I set out to pray more correctly and thoroughly than any person had ever done.

I prayed constantly for Connor and for others. I prayed specifically. I prayed with genuine faith and belief. I prayed with a group of united believers (when two or more are gathered in His name . . . Matthew 18:20). I approached God with a repentant heart, always asking Him to search and find anything that would hinder my prayers. I didn't want to be lacking for anything in my prayer life. I didn't want to find that I was hindering Connor's healing in any way. I found myself following the instructions of all the best books on prayer. I was constantly searching—looking for the right "recipe" for answered prayers.

At the end of Connor's battle with cancer, I was left dazed and confused. Nothing about powerful prayers made sense anymore. The advice from all those "experts" didn't seem to measure up. Even following the Bible's advice on prayer didn't seem to help my case. Neither praying with belief, praying in large numbers, praying specifically, nor praying in the right order had accomplished the goal of having my son healed.

I have come to realize that the course of God's plan for us does not change according to the quality or quantity of our prayers. His plans will not be thwarted. His plans are much bigger than our personal desires. So, here I am searching for the true meaning of my prayers once again. I've come to the conclusion in recent days that our prayers are another example of complete faith and dependence on God's sovereignty without complete understanding. There is no prayer recipe for receiving the answers we want. Instead, our prayerful focus must be upon aligning our will with His. Prayer is an opportunity to commune with Him. It is our grateful response to His blessings and His character. It is our heart's cry of pain and agony that resonates with His heart. It is our choice to be obedient to His commandment to be still and know Him. Prayer is our chance to bask in His presence, to feel His joy and His peace.

I find that all of these lessons continue to bring me back to the same principle . . . complete surrender in all areas of my life. My prayers look different now. I continue to "cast my cares upon Him, because He cares for me" (1 Peter 5:7).

I also like author Sarah Young's perspective on the matter: "Do not seek Me primarily for what I can give you. Remember that I, the Giver, am infinitely greater than any gift I might impart to you. I am calling you to a life of constant communion with Me. Remember your ultimate goal is not to control or fix everything around you; it is to keep communing with Me. A successful day is one in which you have stayed in touch with Me, even if many things remain undone at the end of the day."[4]

God's Silence

As the heavens are higher than the earth, so are My ways
higher than your ways and My thoughts than your thoughts.
—Isaiah 55:9

In the last section, I spoke about not getting the answers for which we have prayed. Sometimes we experience something else with our prayers: God's silence. Countless times when I prayed for my son's healing, I felt there must have been some invisible brick wall between heaven and earth blocking God's answers from reaching me. I would cry out in frustration, "Why can't I hear you?" Other times, when I felt as though I was hearing from God, I thought, *surely I am misunderstanding what He is saying.* Did I have a faulty prayer radar? What do we do when God is silent or unclear?

I do have to say that even when God was silent, I still sensed His presence. I never felt alone. So why is God silent sometimes? Surely, there is a purpose in everything He does. From my perspective now, nine months after Connor's death, I am beginning to understand God's purpose. Recently, when I discussed God's silence in Bible study, a friend made an interesting observation. If the Lord had answered my questions about Connor's fate, how would I have responded? Would I have acted in such faith if I knew Connor would not live past the age of eight? Would I have fought so diligently for him if I had known in advance that my efforts would be in vain? Could I have lived without regrets without that valiant fight for my son's life? Honestly, I don't know the answers to those questions. I do know that things would have been different.

In hindsight, I am grateful for God's silence. Like the Garth Brooks song says, "I'm glad I didn't know the way it all would end." Although it was heart wrenching and maddening at the time, I can now see the wisdom in God's silence. And again, I find that His sovereignty is a blessing. I think His silence is also a form of protection for His children who cannot bear to know all the answers at once. God intends for us to focus on the present moment, where He meets us. He wants us to enjoy His presence moment by moment. We must trust that even when it seems He's not listening, He is still there. We must hold on to Him in the moments when He seems so far away, because nothing can separate us from His love.

My New Hero

The Sovereign LORD is my strength; He makes my feet like
the feet of a deer, He enables me to go on the heights.
—Habakkuk 3:19

I love the Old Testament prophet Habakkuk, who prayed that God would discipline His children, the Israelites, for their sinful behavior. At first, Habakkuk was frustrated because God wasn't answering his prayers. The Israelites continued to sin without repercussion. Then, God finally answered. God told Habakkuk of the destruction coming to Israel at the hands of their enemies, the Babylonians. At first, Habakkuk was in shock. How could God let the Babylonians destroy the Israelites when they were one hundred times more sinful than the Israelites? Surely God could think of a better plan than that! Eventually, Habakkuk accepted God's revelation. In spite of the impending doom at hand, Habakkuk spoke these words in chapter 3:16-19:

> I heard and my heart pounded, my lips quivered at the sound; decay crept into my bones, and my legs trembled. Yet I will wait patiently for the day of calamity to come on the nation invading us. Though the fig tree does not bud and there are no grapes on the vines, though the olive crop fails and the fields produce no food, though there are no sheep in the pen and no cattle in the stalls, yet I will rejoice in the LORD, I will be joyful in God my Savior. The Sovereign LORD is my strength; He makes my feet like the feet of a deer, He enables me to go on the heights.

I'm amazed that Habakkuk could write these words in the face of disaster. He's my new Old Testament hero. I cannot say with confidence that I could have written those words knowing Connor's fate. I guess my God knew that, so He spared me that knowledge beforehand. I pray that we can all say these words from Habakkuk when we are faced with trials, when God is silent, and when we are not rescued from the painful journey we must travel: "yet I will rejoice in the LORD."

Suffering

Dear friends, do not be surprised at the painful trial you are
suffering, as though something strange were happening to you.
But rejoice that you participate in the sufferings of Christ, so
that you may be overjoyed when His glory is revealed.
—1 Peter 4:12-13

As I get older, I have become aware that suffering is a major part of this fallen world. As children, we believe that everything is rosy and that life is full of fairy-tale endings. But now I see that life is also filled with stories that don't match up with the fairy tales I remember.

Life did not look like a fairy tale when our friends lost their one-year-old child to cancer yesterday. Or when my friend's husband left her and her children last year. Or when I think of how many of our friends have lost their jobs and are struggling to support their families. The list goes on. At one time, these everyday trials surprised me, as if they were not a normal part of life. Now, I understand the verse in 1 Peter above.

So what good can come from suffering and how can God's glory be revealed through our pain? Dr. David McKinley, our pastor friend in Augusta, Georgia, has this perspective on suffering:

Suffering forces us to turn from shallow distractions and smaller irritations to consider the ultimate issues in life. It helps us get our eyes on something that really matters. Too much of our time is spent worrying about things that don't matter.

Suffering is the great purifier of the pettiness that often consumes us in life. One of the reasons some of us never develop into people of great character is because we constantly give our attention to the petty things of life. Commentator George Will says "pettiness is the tendency of people without large purposes." If you live with a larger sense of purpose, then you're not going to let your life be burned up by all the little things that really don't matter. This is the spiritual gift of pettiness and pouting. If we ever lose sight of what we are about for eternity—in preaching the gospel, in seeing people redeemed, and helping people who suffer to have a hope and a heaven that is yet to come—then we miss everything that really matters in life and we focus on all the wrong things. That's why Peter says, *"you are tested in the genuineness of your faith, so that it is more precious than gold."* Your life needs to count for more than just the petty trivialities that so often consume us. So suffering in life matters.[5]

I saw this very principle worked out in our lives. When we received Connor's diagnosis, we immediately stopped worrying about the small things. Our minds were wiped clean, and we could finally see what was really important. So, I agree with Pastor McKinley that suffering is the great purifier. Through suffering, we learn not to focus on our troubles or what lies ahead but to only focus on His face. I pray that we can all wipe away all those petty trivialities and focus on what really matters in life—what we are doing for God's kingdom.

When God Says No

> *Your kingdom come, Your will be done, on earth as it is in heaven.*
>
> —Matthew 6:10

Let's face it; no one likes to hear the word *no*. Generally when our five-year-old son Mason receives a no to one of his requests, it is followed by a tantrum or tears. Sometimes he will even say to us, "You don't love me if you won't let me do that. You're not taking good care of me." I laugh to myself when he says those words to me; but, in reality, his thoughts are not so far off from mine with my heavenly Father.

Where do we go when God says no? That's where I stand today. Learning to move past this struggle may be my defining moment. It gives me comfort to know that my Savior also had to deal with God's answer of no. Matthew 26:39 says, "Father, if You are willing, please take this cup of suffering away from me. Yet I want Your will to be done, not mine" (NLT).

Jesus prayed these words when His death on the cross was imminent. Yet, He paused to ask God if there was another way. In life's darkest moments, it is natural to contemplate why God allows us to experience loss. I have struggled with accepting God's comfort to heal my broken heart when He could have spared me this sorrow in the first place. Reading about Jesus' struggle helps me move through my conflict.

"While Jesus was here on earth, He offered prayers and pleadings, with a loud cry and tears, to the One who could rescue Him from death. And God heard His prayers because of His deep reverence for God. Even though Jesus was God's Son, He learned obedience from the things He suffered. In this way, God qualified Him as a perfect High Priest, and He became the source of eternal salvation for all those who obey Him" (Hebrews 5:7-9). I can certainly relate to the prayers and pleadings with loud cries and tears! When God answered no, I thought perhaps He hadn't heard my prayers. This verse assures me that He did. Jesus' reaction to God's answer of no gives me an example to follow in my own life. Like Jesus, I'm trying to learn obedience through suffering. It helps me to know that Jesus wrestled with God's plan for His life and death, even as He submitted to it. Ultimately, He responded to God's answer with, "Not My will, but Yours be done" (Luke 22:42). This is the attitude I'm praying for. I'm standing on a precipice, looking out into my future. I'm holding my plans, my dreams, my pain, my doubt, my loss, and my faith in my hands. The question is: will I surrender all of these before my heavenly Father? Right now, I'm doing it through gritted teeth, but I hope someday it will be with open, willing hand.

This Was Your Best Plan?

Therefore, since Christ suffered In His body, arm yourselves also with the same attitude, because whoever suffers in the body is done with sin. 2 As a result, they do not live the rest of their earthly lives for evil human desires, but rather for the will of God.
—1 Peter 4:1-2

Suffering, the great teacher, has also taught me to look at every situation with a heavenly perspective. It's only normal that we should view life through earthly eyes, but there is so much more to be seen. We often do not recognize God's bigger picture or plan. As I studied Mark 8:31-33 in Sunday school, this became so apparent.

"Jesus began to teach the disciples that the Son of Man must suffer many things and be rejected by the elders, chief priests and teachers of the law, and that he must be killed and after three days rise again. He spoke plainly about this and Peter took Him aside and began to rebuke Him. But when Jesus turned and looked at His disciples, he rebuked Peter. 'Get behind me, Satan! You do not have in mind the things of God, but the things of men.'"

Pretty strong words, aren't they? I tried to imagine what Peter was thinking at that moment. Was he tempted to say to Jesus, "So this is your great plan? You came to earth to *die?* Why don't you just take over your rightful authority on the throne? You are the King of Kings, so use your power to rule here on earth. There has got to be a better way! Why does there have to be a cross?"

I've asked God some of the same questions lately: *So this was your great plan for Connor? There really wasn't a better way? Couldn't Connor have served you better if he were alive?* If I'm not careful, I can become trapped in a vicious cycle of suppositions. Thankfully, in my moments of weakness God always speaks to me from the truth of His Word, "You do not have in mind the things of God, but the things of men" (Mark 8:33).

The world tells us that victory comes through strength instead of weakness, military might rather than selfless surrender, and self-promotion instead of sacrificial submission and humility. I'm sure that was how Peter saw it, but I'm sure his perspective changed when he arrived at the empty tomb. What an "ah-hah" moment that must have been!

When I think of Connor, I wonder if I will have Peter's clarity this side of heaven. Or will the clarity only come when I meet my Savior face to face? I pray that until the answers come, I will continue to cling to my faith and hope in Jesus Christ. As He said in John 21:29, "Because you have seen Me, you have believed; blessed are those who have not seen and yet have believed." I pray that I will focus on the things of God and not the things of man.

God Knows Best

> *Even today, my complaint is bitter; His hand is heavy in*
> *spite of my groaning. If only I knew where to find Him; if*
> *only I could go to His dwelling! I would state my case before*
> *Him and fill my mouth with arguments. I would find out*
> *what He would answer me, and consider what He would*
> *say . . . My feet have closely followed His steps; I have kept*
> *to His way without turning aside. I have not departed from*
> *the commands of His lips; I have treasured the words of His*
> *mouth more than my daily bread. But He stands alone, and*
> *who can oppose Him? He does whatever He pleases.*
>
> —Job 23:2-5, 11-13

I understand the frustration Job expresses in the verses above. We
so often convince ourselves that if we live a life that follows after
Christ, we should receive whatever we ask for in prayer. It makes
no sense that others are rewarded for unrighteous behavior, while
righteous men like Job don't get their prayers answered. It seems so
unfair. Several times since Connor's death, I have cried out to God
in my frustration. *Did I not glorify you in my trials? Did I not exhibit*
faith in you at all times? Shouldn't I be rewarded for my efforts? I have
seen other families battling childhood cancer who make no mention
of God but continue to hold their surviving children in their arms.
It makes no sense and doesn't seem fair.

God's response to Job really changed my perspective:

> "Who is this that darkens counsel by words without
> knowledge? Now gird up your loins like a man and I will
> ask you, and you instruct Me! Where were you when I
> laid the earth's foundation? Tell me, if you understand.
> Who marked off its dimensions? Surely you know! Who
> stretched a measuring line across it? On what were
> its footings set, or who laid its cornerstone while the
> morning stars sang together and all the angels shouted
> for joy?" (Job 38:2-7).

God's words remind me of my common response to my children: "Because I said so." Better yet is Bill Cosby's line: "I brought you into this world, and I can take you out." I can see that God doesn't have to defend His actions to me. He's the one and only true God, and He put this world into motion. He's my creator and my Lord. I owe Him my total allegiance and love, not my questions and accusations.

Guilt No More

All the days Ordained for me were written in Your book before
one of them came to be.

—Psalm 139:16

Several times over the past year, I have struggled with feelings of regret. I know it is the normal progression of grief to second-guess our attempts at saving our loved one. And yet, in quiet moments, "what if" becomes a daunting, taunting mantra in my head. *What if Connor had never had radiation? What if we had gone to another hospital for treatment? What if we had found the second cancer sooner?* The list of questions goes on and on, leaving me with little peace. I know that we fought long and hard for our son. I do not regret any of our actions, but I experienced a period of worrying that I may have misread God's guidance. Did I miss something God was trying to tell me? Did I fail to obey Him when He gave me instruction?

Once again, God revealed His perfect answer to me, this time from Psalm 139:

O LORD, you have searched me and you know me.
You know when I sit and when I rise;
    you perceive my thoughts from afar.
You discern my going out and my lying down;
    you are familiar with all my ways.
Before a word is on my tongue you know it completely,
    O LORD.
You hem me in—behind and before; you have laid your
    hand upon me.
Such knowledge is too wonderful for me, too lofty for
    me to attain.
Where can I go from your Spirit?
Where can I flee from your presence?
If I go up to the heavens, you are there;
    if I make my bed in the depths, you are there.
If I rise on the wings of the dawn,

if I settle on the far side of the sea,
Even there your hand will guide me, your right hand will
   hold me fast. For you created my inmost being;
you knit me together in my mother's womb.
I praise you because I am fearfully and wonderfully
   made;
   your works are wonderful,I know that full well.
My frame was not hidden from you
   when I was made in the secret place.
When I was woven together in the depths of the earth,
   your eyes saw my unformed body.
All the days ordained for me were written in your book
   before one of them came to be.

Reading these verses reminded me of God's protective hand on our lives. No matter what mistakes we made, God had Connor's life planned for him years before he was even created, before the beginning of time. I've read Psalm 139 many times through the years, but this time it provided a much-needed release from my guilt. It's not what I did or didn't do that determined Connor's fate. If you have felt the burden of responsibility for a loved one's welfare, you know the weight of your decisions is staggering. We have to remember that God is in control. He knows the direction you will take. He knows every consequence and ripple effect. Let this knowledge relieve you of any stress or guilt that you may have.

Gonna Be Worth It

*For our light and momentary troubles are achieving for us an
eternal glory that far outweighs them all.*
—2 Corinthians 4:17

When Connor was battling cancer, especially during his last six months, it would just kill me to see him suffer. I felt the suffering right along with him. My heart actually ached when I looked at his sweet face and his body wasting away before my eyes. I think that was really when I questioned God the most. *How can you let this sweet child suffer like this?* It was inhumane. I have often thought to myself that one of my first questions to Jesus when I see Him will be "why such suffering?" And then, I wonder if I'll still care about that when I finally see His face. Will all of those thoughts and pains just disappear at the sight of Him? I imagine it's like forgetting the pains of childbirth once you hold your child in your arms. The song "It's Gonna Be Worth It All" by Rita Springer is about this very thing—how our earthly troubles will be worth it when we see His face.

To quote Corinthians 4:17 again, "For our light and momentary troubles are achieving for us an eternal glory that far outweighs them all." I wish I could have been there when Connor saw Jesus for the first time. I'm sure that the pain and discomfort he had been feeling for those last several months were all forgotten at the sight of His face. I'm sure Connor felt it was all worth it . . . just to see His face!

In Revelation, John speaks of the coming tribulations and suffering of Christians for the sake of Jesus' name. He encourages them all to be conquerors in these trials, and they will receive a reward beyond their comprehension. The reward will be worth the cost. "Do not fear what you are about you suffer. Behold, the devil is about to throw some of you into prison, that you may be tested, and you will have tribulation. Be faithful unto death, and I will give you the crown of life . . . The one who conquers, I will grant him to sit with Me on My throne" (Revelations 2:10, 3:21). I can just hear Connor whispering to me, "Mom, it's gonna be worth it!"

The Coming Dawn

I will turn their mourning into gladness; I will give them comfort and joy instead of sorrow . . . Restrain your voice from weeping and your eyes from tears, for your work will be rewarded. So there is hope for your future, declares the Lord.
—Jeremiah 31:13, 16

I've been trying to sum up how I feel about the first anniversary of Connor's entry into heaven. It's hard to endure the pain I feel and yet still focus on the hope I have in Christ. As July 10 approaches, Tait and I are remembering the days that led up to Connor's passing. These memories are filled with Connor's pain and suffering—it is difficult to revisit them.

One day, as I sat quietly in reflection, it was like Connor spoke to me and said, "Mom, I'm not like that anymore. I am not suffering or in pain. Don't put yourself through that misery anymore. You're going through unnecessary pain, because those days are over for me. Why put yourself through that?" So, I'm taking Connor's advice. I'm focusing on a new beginning—a new dawn. I'm counting on God's promises to restore joy to our lives. "The sufferings of this present time are not worthy to be compared with the glory that is to be revealed to us" (Romans 8:18). Our pain and struggles are very real, but they are only the dark before the morning.

It's like what our pastor, Jack Graham, said at Connor's service. "Don't trade what you do know for what you don't know." I don't know why this had to happen to Connor—why he had to get two cancers by the age of eight and why he had to die. I may never know those answers this side of heaven, but I do know a lot of things about God. He loves us, He will never leave us, He died for us, and He prepared a place in heaven for those who love Him. I will choose to focus on what I do know and the dawn. Someday, I will see Connor again, and God's glory will be revealed to me. That is the promise to which I cling. Until that day, I will fight the good fight, as Connor would have wanted me to.

Final Words

We know that in all things God works for the good of those who
love Him, who have been called according to His purpose.
—Romans 8:28

My heart overflows with gratitude and love for all of you who faithfully prayed for my son over the last four years and now continue to pray for my family as we heal. The outpouring of love and support has been incredible. Thank you for honoring my son's life. Your words of encouragement and stories of how Connor touched your lives have brought us such comfort as we have walked through these difficult days. We cannot thank you enough.

I will continue to share how God is carrying us through this dark valley and how He is redeeming this situation. That is what He does, isn't it? He brings good out of bad. He brings water to the desert and joy to our sadness. Our eyes and hearts are open to what He is accomplishing in our lives.

I wanted to share this letter that I wrote to Connor. One paragraph was read during his memorial service, but here is the letter in its entirety.

Dear Connor, my valiant warrior,

I know, as a mother, I am supposed to be the one who teaches her children, who imparts wisdom and insight for life. How is it then that you were the one who taught me? You taught me how to enjoy life, with your radiant smile, your silly ways, and your happy dance. You were always looking for an adventure, whether it was dodge ball in the back yard with your family or sword fighting with your friends in our fort or races in the halls of the hospital. Nothing could contain your love of life.

You taught me how to love. No one could pass by you without a hug from "Con-Con." You had a love that was irrepressible; it overflowed and was passed out to others as easily as you breathed. It was as if you knew you only had a short time with us, so you had to send out all your love in just eight and a half years. Oh, how you made us feel special.

You taught me how to fight valiantly. How many times have I watched you suffer bravely through pain that would have caused most people to quit? How many times were you knocked down, only to rise stronger the next time? You were so tenacious, never giving up. Even in the end, your body gave up before your fighting spirit did. You had the heart of a lion. You amazed the doctors from Dallas, Boston, New York, Houston, and even Guatemala. How many times was your prognosis not good, yet you continued your battle without a falter in your step? What a brave warrior you were. How could I not fight so hard for you, when your spirit was so strong?

You taught me how to dance in the rain. Although half of your life was spent battling this disease, cancer, you never let it stop you from enjoying life. You never made room for complaining. You would be healing from surgery or recovering from chemotherapy, and you would still show up at baseball practice. You wanted to experience it all. Nothing stopped you from absorbing all the joy possible. Even in your last week with us, you went to Gatti Town, to see *Ice Age*, to the bookstore, to the Lego™ store, and to your favorite restaurant. Your motto was, "Live, enjoy, cherish!"

You taught me about faith and loving your heavenly Father. You never once questioned God's goodness during this journey. You always expected healing to come. You knew your Father would never leave you nor forsake you. You wanted to tell the world about Jesus. Your words of encouragement to others battling cancer were, "Have courage, and believe in Jesus." That says it all. And that's what you did. You walked your talk.

I know that we have all said that you lost your battle with cancer last Friday. But, as I think about it, I realize you actually won the battle. We often think it is a tragedy when one so young passes away, but maybe we are looking at this all wrong. I think your reward, my sweet son, for your faithful, brave battle is that you are now dancing on golden streets in heaven, holding Jesus' hand. You have shed the pain and struggles that accompany a life on this earth, and you are now rejoicing with the angels and feeling love like you've never known. How can that be a battle lost? Well done, my good and faithful son. We love you and will miss you. Enjoy your well-earned reward!

Love, Mom

Tait wrote this reflection and letter to Connor nine months after Connor was diagnosed with the initial tumor in 2004.

Nine months ago almost to the day this started, and oh what I have learned so far:

1. God is in charge, and we are in the stands watching. That is such a good feeling. It is not in our hands. It is all in our sovereign Lord's hands. There is nothing we can do but pray and remain faithful.
2. Enjoy your children to the minute, because they are on loan from God.

Dear Connor,

As you lie in that bed for another night (day twenty-seven), it's hard to close the house down without you. Each time I kiss you goodbye or goodnight, I whisper in your ear, "Fight Connor; fight for life." Remember the mornings with eggs cooking and the smell of Grandmas coffee. Connor, remember the feel of a freshly washed shirt, and the smell of Mommy's car on the way to school with the music on and everyone talking so loud. Connor, remember your school and the cool playground and all your friends there, such as Ann Renee. Connor, remember church and praying to God with the taste of doughnuts in your mouth and the feeling of a hug from your mom and me as we drop you off at your Sunday school class; remember your excitement when you see your buddy, Mollie Claire.

Remember the anticipation of waking up Christmas morning and running down the stairs with your siblings to see your Christmas presents. Connor, remember the smell of Mexican food and the burn of a Coke in your mouth. Remember naps with Daddy and the feeling of the fresh grass as we wrestle for hours. Connor, remember the snap of the plastic swords as we fight and attack each other's forts. Remember your brother, Carson, and his love for you; remember the hours of playing with him. Remember hugs from Mommy, Grandma, and Aunt Cody and tickle fights with Cousin Lexie.

Connor, remember the feeling of the hot tub as it bubbles with the steam in your nose before we go to eat at Tin Star or the Purple Cow. Connor, remember Mackenzie and all her fun, smiles, and laughs as you two play, watch TV, or go with whatever she wants. Remember Mason our sweet little baby and your fun Uncle Tom, Grandpa Burt, Mitch, Trent, Kylie, and Chasie Boo. Connor, remember the hot summer sun, your bike, the yellow gator, the rides in the Land Rover to Sonic, fishing at our ranch, the big giraffe in our house, the rides in Grandpa's tractor looking for deer, and the super fast car rides with all the windows down in Daddy's car. Connor, remember the fun times sitting in Grandpa's lap, listening to Daddy's loud music, and visiting Uncle Rod's business, Rodman Excavation, where you get to play on all the cool bulldozers. Connor, remember Slurpees and nachos and cheese sticks and Mommy telling you to eat your veggies. Connor, remember family nights and adventures on your motorcycle with Brittney and Carson. Remember our wonderful house with snow on the roof; remember the feeling of rain and smell of spring and wind in your face.

Connor, remember the sound of a basketball or the slap of a soccer ball and all those fun nights with Daddy at the Stars games. Connor, remember playing hide and seek with your friend Cade next door and the feeling of losing your breath as you run away. Connor, remember movies, Spongebob Squarepants, and baths with Carson.

Connor, don't look back and let time stand still. It's time to live and go forward and see the people who love you and your friends who surround you. Remember your dream to go back to Disney World? Dream of playing on the beach and hunting in Africa with Daddy and Grandpa. Dream of playing football and basketball, driving a car, and your first concert. Dream of being baptized and shooting your first deer; dream of your first kiss and the dizzy-wonderful feeling when your bride walks down the aisle to marry you. Connor, we are all ready for you to come home and be cancer free. Connor, I love you.

Daddy

Notes

Chapter 1

1. William Williams and John Hughes, "Guide Me O Thou Great Jehovah," www.hymnsite.com.
2. Alfred Edersheim, *The Amazing Collection: Esther* (Colorado Springs: NavPress, 2005).
3. Oswald Chambers, "The Graciousness of Uncertainty" (April 29), *My Utmost for His Highest* (Grand Rapids, MI: Discovery House, 1992).
4. Sarah Young, *Jesus Calling* (Nashville: Thomas Nelson, 2004).

Chapter 2

1. Beth Moore, *Believing God* (Nashville: B&H Books, 2004).
2. Frances J. Roberts, *On the High Road of Surrender* (Uhrichsville, OH: Barbour, 2004).

Chapter 3

1. Frances J. Roberts, *On the High Road of Surrender* (Uhrichsville, OH: Barbour, 2004).

Chapter 4

1. Dr. Jack Graham, Prestonwood Baptist Church, www. prestonwoodbaptistchurch.org.
2. Dr. James C. Dobson, *In the Arms of God* (Carol Stream, IL: Tyndale House, 1997).
3. Stormy Omartian, *The Power of a Praying Parent* (Eugene, OR: Harvest House, 1995).
4. Frances J. Roberts, *On the High Road of Surrender* (Uhrichsville, OH: Barbour Publishing, 2004).

Chapter 5

1. Joni Eareckson Tada, *Pearls of Great Price* (Grand Rapids, MI: Zondervan, 2006).
2. Beth Moore, *Believing God* (Nashville: B&H Books, 2004).
3. James Denison, see www.godissues.org.
4. Chuck Swindoll, *Be Still*.
5. Frances J. Roberts, *On the High Road of Surrender* (Uhrichsville, OH: Barbour, 2004).

Chapter 6

1. Oswald Chambers, *The Amazing Collection: Esther*, NavPress (Colorado Springs: NavPress, 2005).

Chapter 8

1. Dr. Alan Redpath, see www.dailychristianquote.com.
2. Frances J. Roberts, *On the High Road of Surrender* (Uhrichsville, OH: Barbour, 2004).
3. Ibid.
4. Sarah Young, *Jesus Calling* (Nashville: Thomas Nelson, 2004).
5. Dr. David McKinley, Warren Baptist Church, Augusta, Georgia. www.davidhmckinley.com

Epilogue

My goal in writing Hope Transformed was to give you, the reader, a glimpse into my family's journey with Connor so you would understand how God carried us through this difficult trial. I hope that our story becomes a tool to help you through your own difficult journeys. Knowing that our hope must be in an authentic relationship with Christ and not His ability to remove the pain from our circumstances kept us centered on Christ even when we felt disappointed with God. I pray that our story awakened new perspectives on God's love and faithfulness in your life, a perspective that stays with you long after the trial is over.

If Hope Transformed challenged you, encouraged you, or transformed your hope in Christ, please share our story with others. A simple step would be to give this book to people you care about. It may help them to feel less alone and it may give them hope. It may begin a deeper conversation about faith and what a relationship with Christ is truly about.

If you are willing to join me in spreading the message of hope in this book, visit our book website www.hopetransformed. com<HYPERLINK "http://www.hopetransformed.com/"http://www. hopetransformed.com> and order a pack of ten books to distribute to your friends and family. A percentage of the profits from the sale of this book will go directly to our charity, The Team Connor Childhood Cancer Foundation, which raises funds for pediatric cancer treatment and cure research, and promotes awareness of this devastating disease. For more information, please visit www.

teamconnor.org<HYPERLINK "http://www.teamconnor.org/"http://
www.teamconnor.org>

Thanks in advance for your support and for joining us on our
mission to spread eternal hope to others.

Always believing,

Joy Cruse

About the Authors

Joy and Tait Cruse are the proud parents of Mackenzie, Carson, Mason, and Connor (who now resides in heaven). Throughout Connor's four-year battle with neuroblastoma, Joy wrote a blog on a website called caringbridge which served as the inspiration for this book. Her corresponding blog, "Joy's Journal," continues to be followed by thousands of people throughout the world. Joy and Tait are the founders of Team Connor, a 501 c-3 that raises money to support childhood cancer research. To learn more about Connor Cruse, neuroblastoma, or Team Connor, please visit www.teamconnor.org.

Made in the USA
Lexington, KY
03 February 2012